Manipulation And Body Language

THE COMPLETE GUIDE TO THE
ART OF PERSUASION, DISCOVER
THINGS ABOUT DARK
PSYCHOLOGY AND LEARN HOW
TO READ AND INFLUENCE
PEOPLE BY ANALYZING BODY
LANGUAGE

JIM BUIRTER

Legal Notice:

This book is copyright protected. This book is only for personal use.
You cannot amend, distribute, sell, use, quote or paraphrase any
part, or the content within this book, without the consent of the
author or publisher.

Disclaimer Notice:

Please note the information contained within this document is for
educational and entertainment purposes only. All effort has been
executed to present accurate, up to date, and reliable, complete
information. No warranties of any kind are declared or implied.
Readers acknowledge that the author is not engaging in the
rendering of legal, financial, medical or professional advice. The
content within this book has been derived from various sources.
Please consult a licensed professional before attempting any
techniques outlined in this book.

By reading this document, the reader agrees that under no
circumstances is the author responsible for any losses, direct or
indirect, which are incurred as a result of the use of information
contained within this document, including, but not limited to, -
errors, omissions, or inaccuracies.

TABLE OF CONTENTS

INTRODUCTION

When wetalk about covert manipulation, we talk about a kind of manipulation that happensbelow the conscious awareness level. If you are a target of this type of manipulation, you probably, will not be aware of what is going on, which makes it the most difficult type of manipulation to spot and deal with.

Some of the most skilled manipulators will be able to make you doubt your emotional welfare and self-worth, which makes it easier for them to control you. When you fall into this trap, the manipulator is able to take away your identity and your self-esteem. This takes a lot of time to accomplish, but then they have time to get you to do what they want.

Most experts will refer to these skilled manipulators as covert-aggressive people. They will have a tactical belt of tools that can use to get the target. Usually, they are so skilled that you will fall without even noticing. Some of the tactics that a covert manipulator will use includes:

• The ability to hide their aggressive intentions,

• Make you afraid, doubt yourself, and more, until you are willing to give in to them.

Dangerous manipulators

The best emotional manipulators can use almost any type of behavior to accomplish their goals. They are even more dangerous when they read behavioral patterns and the actions of the target. When they can read the target, they will soon know the target inside and out, such as the level of conscientiousness, weaknesses, fears, insecurities, and beliefs. And in the hands of a manipulator, knowledge is power that they can use against their target.

In some cases, the manipulator can even know as a psychopath. There are many manipulators who don't fall into this category, but still, it's very difficult to have a real relationship with a manipulator.Take a lot of time to study people, and also will never think twice to use this information against the target. They are more concerned about being able to get what they want in every situation that will not stop to consider the target's feelings or how they should be acting in a real relationship.

The main factor that you need to keep in mind is manipulators need to be in control.They hunger for power and will do whatever they need to achieve that goal. They will often hurt people in the process, and it will not bother them at all. If you ever feel that you are less superior, less intelligent, less strong, or less confident in your life, especially if you are with a specific person; so, this person may be manipulating you.

Think about the relationship that you have right now. Are you able to remember back when you met? Was it something magical, something that swept you off your feet? You will find that most manipulators are sweet talkers. They are adept at hidingtheir real personalities and real plans from their target. They already have plans to trick you to get what they want, and they will start from the first moment that they meet you.

In the beginning, this person will make you believe that they are willing to do anything for you, and they will keep up with this act until you are hooked deeply, and until you show them your vulnerability. Once you have done this, they will start to bring out the manipulation, and sometimes the extreme abuse will start if you let it.

Over time, usually pretty slowly, so it is hard to pinpoint when it actually started, you will be able to notice that your ideal relationship has changed. It has become more confusing, exploitative, and demeaning. You will notice that the self-esteem that you had at the beginning (whether it was strong or not) will start to turn into doubt, and it is likely that you will start to blame yourself for this issue.

At this time, the manipulator will have full control. It will not be long until you are fine with just getting crumbs out of all the interactions in the relationship. You will be blamed for everything that goes wrong, even if you had nothing to do with it. You will have to take care of all their needs and care about them all the time, while they will no longer care about you or your fears, needs, and emotions. These manipulators do not really care about any of these things; they only pretend to care at the beginning to get you hooked on them.

It is amazing how quickly things can change. Once a target is under the control of their manipulator, even those with very high self-esteem will turn it around. They will start to blame themselves for anything and everything that goes wrong in the relationship. They will start to over-analyze things that happen in their lives, and usually, they will do this until they are so confused that they do not know what is going on in their lives. Every part of their day can start to suffer because of this confusion and the tactics of the manipulator, such as their mental health, physical health, social relationships, and career.

The sad part about all of this is that the manipulator will be able to do all of this without you seeing where it started. It is not something that happens one day, and then you can see it and leave. It starts out slowly, usually with a few little remarks or tactics that are used. Then one day, the manipulator will have taken over all the control, and you don't know how to handle the issue at all or to understand what is going on.

CHAPTER - 1

WHAT IS MANIPULATION

Manipulation deals with using your actions, mannerisms, hands, and even other parts of your body to get someone to do what you want, or to sharpen a situation to your desire. You could think of it as being selfish, but I tell you that in every wrongdoing, there is a drive. Therefore, the drive behind manipulation could be positively used. An instance can be seen in how a good DJ tries to bring different styles of music together to display its skills in bringing many tunes together into a lovely mix of sounds to the audience. We could say this is almost unfair to the original artist of each song. Also, someone that is good at manipulating would know how to do so in words, emotions, and feelings to the very end of getting his or her main desire.

The practice of manipulation could involve the use of an indirect scheme and plan to be in charge of relationships. Periodic manipulation involves telling a friend that he or she is looking well when the person is actually mentally depressed or/and physically down. This is quite technical as it will affect your friend's perceptions of you, which will eventually translate to how the person relates to you. Emotional abuse can be associated with manipulation, especially when it is experienced in very close relationships. Depending on the point of view, someone can consider manipulation negative when the person being manipulated is affected physically, emotionally, or mentally while another person can argue that because being manipulative helps to put one's surroundings and environment, including people into subjection and under control. Moreover, manipulators could find it hard to connect with their original selves, and being manipulated can lead to ill effects in an individual.

To understand manipulation, you have to identify the major three distinct types. First, we have manipulation of options in which the options available in the environment are modified by rewards or threats. The second one is the manipulation of information; here, the individual's way of perceiving things is modified such that the understanding of the situation gets affected. Also, psychological manipulation is a process of influencing someone such that there is a change in mental cognition.

During manipulative encounters, there are four main components of manipulations, which are hearer, motive, covertness, and interest of the speaker. These are usually referred to as prerequisites to manipulation. Any form of manipulation is geared towards affecting a hearer or victim. The target often times, will behave in such a way to oppose how he acts before being manipulated. Actually, in a manipulative situation, the manipulator has a larger vision spectrum, which means that the manipulator knows much better than the target.

Talking about motive, is this not what characterizes manipulation itself? The intention of the speaker determines to what extent the target is manipulated. However, this intention cannot be known to the hearer else; it would be self-defeating. There is usually a communication involving the hearer, the speaker, and the speaker's communicated motives.

For the widespread view on manipulation to hold, it then needs to remain covert. I can assume, to a large extent, that the motive of the speaker is one important feature in manipulation. It is actually designed to suit the desire and interest of the speaker. I can also tell you that there is a correlation between a manipulative mechanism and the motive of the manipulator.

Now, it is imperative to know that manipulations can be done unconsciously or without being aware, while some people manipulate deliberately. Intentional manipulators are tricky in nature. They would even brag of what they do because they are very much aware. The game known as manipulation enables manipulators to be wise, smart, and cunny at the same time. They are also self-centered, so you cannot claim to be good at manipulating and care for others.

Various forms of manipulation include

Unintentional resistance to the demands of others can be making excuses, blaming others, sarcasm, hiding anger, among others.

Indirect or Implied Threats. An example of this is when, as a mother, you give your child a bad look for leaving its dirty uniform on the floor.

Deceitfulness in character or behavior includes cheating, fabrication, corruption, and even stealing.

Selfishness in disseminating useful information. For example, let's suppose that you and your friend need a new job,and when you get information about companies having vacancies, you hold it back from your friend.

Achieving a goal via sexual intercourse. This is common among employers and employees.

However, if manipulation is not being addressed, people who are being manipulated can suffer from poor mental health. Chronic manipulation could result in depression, anxiety, wrong coping methods, lying, and difficulty in trusting people. Also, it could make a victim lose his or her value system, and doubt things in their real sense. An instance was illustrated in a classic movie titled "Gaslight," wherein a subtly manner, the husband of a woman manipulated her until she no longer depends on how she perceives things. The man secretly turned down the gaslights, and he made his wife believe that the way the light looks dim was all in her head.

Manipulators are also good at saying sweet things their victim would like, and most words from them are not all that true. They take advantage of being skilled in this to develop a close and amazing connection with people. A manipulator will deliberately create an imbalanced way of using a victim to their advantage. Until such a person gets what he/she wants, they can go to any length.

There are some subtly behavior that when you sense them either from you or others, you should smell manipulation. Instances include acting dumb and pretending to be nice and lovely all the time. Really, if we all what to be truthful, at a point or the other in our lives, we have been manipulative. Sometimes, to control people, tell a lie so as to get out of a situation or even to flatter. To some people, it is a way of life.

As you know, or have even experienced, manipulators are everywhere. The question should be, what personalities do they possess? A manipulator could be your neighbor who spreads gist and gossip about you. They could even be your family members who make people around them feel insecure or who always create chaos, so in the end, anybody could actually manipulate you. On the road, manipulators are usually criminals who rely on gimmicks to distract you in order to take your belongings.

They can also exist at your workplace as someone who doesn't mind stepping on everybody's toe just to get what they what. What they want to include power, promotion, salary, and feeling superior, so really it is not that they are emotionally strong but weak. A manipulator would even make the life of other colleagues miserable and keep upsetting them as long as he wants. They rely more on being secrecy.

Manipulation can come in any shape from the least expected person. You should know that those who manipulate people tend to suffer from a personality disorder. They might have odd responses to situations because of how the reason. These individuals might even have to display emotional and behavioral difficulties quite strange from that of the families they belong to.

Psychological manipulation is an example of social influence that aims at changing other people's mindsets through an indirect, deceptive, or underhanded ways. This method can be considered as being devious and exploitative. Most times, social influence is not negative. For instance, when you have a bad habit, people around you, such as your doctor, family, or even friends, try to persuade you to change. This kind of manipulation is considered harmless; this is because the person has a right to reject or accept.

You can manipulate someone's emotions by influencing how the other person thinks, behave, or respond to circumstances and situation in a manner that suits what you want. The behavior of a manipulator usually varies from situation to situation, depending on what is at stake. They can speak in a rude manner, and in the following minute, they can act extremely nicely. Sometimes, you really might not be able to tell when such a person is manipulative.

CHAPTER - 2

METHODS OF MANIPULATION

Falsifying Confusion: The manipulative individual attempts to feign stupidly by falsely claiming no recollection of what the victim is speaking about or recalling or that this is the first-time hearing about a major problem being brought to their attention. Confusing the person is what the manipulator will do so that the person doubts their own precision of interpretation, often pointing out important aspects that the manipulator deliberately included in the event of dispute.

Being acquainted with people who will assist them in advance may be used sometimes by manipulators to help back up their story and seem reliable.

Brandishing Anger: The manipulative individual utilizes rage towards the victim in order to shake them into submission with adequate mental force and rage. Actually, the manipulator isn't upset, they just wanted to make a performance. This was simply what the manipulator wanted, to get "upset" when refused or called out. Planned rage, or anger is often used as a manipulating technique to avoid conflict. False rage is also exercised to dodge having to be honest about the situation or event, or maybe to further hide purpose. The manipulator frequently utilizes threats to reach officials, or mistakenly reports abuses which the manipulative schemer has intentionally produced in order to threaten or intimidate the person to comply. Threats, in particular if the victim accepts initial requests or suggestions by manipulators. Using anger as a defense is a way of avoiding the manipulation of anger to be honest in uncomfortable times or circumstances. Anger as a distracting strategy is often used to misdirect investigations or suspects. When a manipulator uses this tactic, the accuser is distracted and is more concerned about the anger brought upon by the manipulator.

Bandwagon Effect: The manipulator may subtly coax the victim into compliance by claiming that many people already have done something, and the victim should as well, even if the claim is true or false. They will use phrases like "Many people like you" or "Everyone does this anyways." The manipulator uses this tactic as a form of peer pressure for certain situations in which the manipulator is trying to influence the victim into trying things that are against the victim's better judgement, such as trying drugs or other substances.

The following vulnerabilities that may occur in victims are exploited by manipulators:

the "People pleasing". Addiction to other people's consent and recognition. This includes aversion to negative behavior, or emetophobia, which is the fear or aversion or fear of adverse emotions.

lack of confidence and inability to disagree, for fear of not being liked. A weak logic of self, such as lax individual personal limits.

lax dependence in self. A person who believes that they have complete control over situations in their lives.

The previous vulnerabilities that may occur in offenders are exploited by manipulators:

- naïveté – This can be where the victim realizes the difficulty to accept the concept or idea that if they are affected by the manipulator. Some individuals are smart, devious and cruel or are "in isolation."

- over-meticulousness – Targeted individual is too sympathetic and is ready to profit from trust and to see the angle of the manipulator and relate to where they fault the targeted individual.

- less-confidence in one's self - Here the victim lacks trust and determination and doubts about himself, and is probably, if readily challenged, get defensive rather simply.

- over-thinking - This is where the victim tries very hard to sympathize and relate to the manipulator and can see some empathetic reason for them to be hurtful.

- emotional dependency – the person targeted can have a dependent or submissive character. The more susceptible the person is, the better utilized and exploited.

Manipulators will generally make the time to analyze the characteristics and vulnerabilities of their victims.

Noted psychiatrist J.R Kantor advises that psychopathic manipulators are attracted to certain vulnerabilities of their victims who are too:

- Dependent – So they can say ' yes ' to something, which they ought to say ' no, ' depending on a need to be liked.

- Immature – They tend to believe exaggerated advertising claims, based on impaired judgment.

- Naïve – Takes it for granted that if there are any dishonest people in the world, they will not be allowed to prey on others. Refuse to believe there are dishonest people.

- Impressionable – People who are easily seduced and taken advantage of by charmers. Politicians influence these people by being seemingly charming by kissing babies to gain votes.

- Trusting – They often assume that everyone else is honest, because they are honest. If the manipulator gains its favor, they are more enthusiastic about engaging with people they don't know without reviewing any qualifications or backgrounds and less willing to examine their personal past or reputation.

- Carelessness – Not giving a specific amount of time to understand or acknowledge harm to others or to themselves.

- Lonely – A person psychopathic can give personal accompaniment for a cost that is accepted by lonely individuals.

- Narcissistic – Being prone to flattery, a manipulator may use this.

- Impulsive – Will make instant judgements

and decisions without giving rational thought, usually without consulting others.

- Altruistic - They may be too fair or too empathetic to a fault. They do things without hope for reward.

- Frugal – Will be attentive to good deals or bargains. They will be attracted to things that are cheap.

- Materialistic – They see worth and value in what is tangible. They can be susceptible to loan sharks or schemes to get rich quick.

- Greedy–They may be enticed by a psychopath into doing something possibly dangerous or immoral for financial or material gain.

- Masochistic – They let psychopaths' benefit, because they believe that they merit it out of a feeling of guilt and probable disregard for themselves.

- The elderly – They can be prone to giving charity because they can become fatigued and, if bombarded with a sudden sales pitch, are less capable of making sudden decisions in their old age.

Manipulators can be motivated by different reasons, such as, but not limited to:

Personal gain at virtually any cost. They are used to advance their own purposes without fear of consequences.

They need authority and supremacy over connections that are abnormally powerful.

A want and need to feel and be in control and power. They want to gain power over others so that they can boost their feeling of self-worth.

Seeing their surroundings more as a game. This cause for them to be manipulative may come from bored of their surroundings motivation by secret personal agendas, criminal or otherwise.

Manipulating using a sphere of influence or deception, such as in financial manipulation of the elderly (unprotected wealthy are targeted intentionally for the sole purpose of obtaining the financial assets).

Manipulation Techniques

Lying is one of the very first techniques that manipulators use. It is a technique that pathological liars or psychopaths use when they want to confuse their victims. If they are constantly lying to them, their victims will often be unaware of the truth. Those who use this tactic have no moral or ethical apprehension about it.

Telling half-truths or only telling part of a story is another tactic that can be used to manipulate someone. People like this will often keep things to themselves because it puts the victim at a disadvantage. They can get what they want by waiting to tell them the rest of the story until their needs are met.

Being around someone who has frequent mood swings can often make a person vulnerable to their manipulations. Not knowing what mood that person will be in, whether they will be happy, sad, or angry can be a very useful tactic for the manipulator. It keeps the victim off balance and easy to manipulate because they will often do what the manipulator wants to keep them in a good mood.

Another tactic that is often used by narcissists is known as love bombing. This doesn't necessarily mean that you have to be in a relationship but can be used in a friendship as well. Those that use this tactic will charm the victim to death and have them believe that this is the best relationship or friendship that has ever happened to them. They will use the victim for what they want, and then when they are done, they drop them and the victim has no idea what happened.

A tactic that can be used in extreme cases by the manipulator is that of punishment. This makes the victim feel guilty for something they did wrong, even if they didn't do anything at all. Some of the punishments that they can inflict on their victims are consistent nagging, shouting, mental abuse, giving them the silent treatment, and even as bad as physical violence.

Denial is often a tactic that is used when a manipulator feels pushed in a corner, and they feel like they will be exposed for the fake that they are. In this instance, they will manipulate the victim into believing that they are doing the very thing the manipulator is being accused of.

Spinning the truth is a tactic often used by politicians. It is used to twist the facts to suit their needs or wants. Sociopaths use this technique to disguise their bad behavior and justify it to their victims.

Minimizing is when a manipulator will play down their behavior and/or actions. They move the blame onto the victim for overreacting when their actions are harmful, and the person has a valid reason for feeling the way they do.

It is often interesting when the manipulator pretends to become the victim. They do this to gain sympathy or compassion from their real victims. They do this so that their victims feel a sense of responsibility to help and end their suffering, especially if they feel that they are the cause of that person's suffering.

Another way that the manipulator can move the blame onto the victim is by targeting the victim and accusing them of wrongdoing. The victim will then start to defend themselves, while the manipulator hides their manipulation away from the victim. This can be dangerous because the victim is so focused on defending themselves that they forget to notice what is right in front of them.

Using the positive reinforcement tactic tricks the victim into thinking that they are getting something for helping the manipulator get what they want. This can be through purchasing them expensive presents, praising them, giving them money, constantly apologizing for their behavior, giving them lots of attention and all-around buttering them up.

There are times when a person knows where they stand with someone. However, in any type of relationship, the manipulator might keep moving the goal just to confuse their victim because they thought that everyone was still on the same page.

CHAPTER - 3

DEVELOPING STAGES
OF MANIPULATION

Causes of Manipulation

Exercising undue influence on others using mental distortion or emotional exploitation with the sole intention of gaining power and control over the victim and at the victim's expense is known as psychological manipulation. Before learning about becoming a master manipulator, you must learn to differentiate between positive social influence and psychological manipulation. Strong social forces are not only crucial for a good and constructive relationship but are also based on the concept of 'give and take. '

On the other hand, a psychological manipulator exploits his victims to get what he wants. There exist elements of power imbalances in a relationship when it comes to psychological manipulation. There are four common traits of manipulative individuals.

They are good at detecting others' weaknesses.

Once they identify such weaknesses, they will use them against the person.

Manipulative individuals are quite intelligent and will influence others to do what they want to meet their self-oriented goals.

Once a manipulator gets hold of his victim, the manipulation will go on until the victim stops him or until the manipulator loses interest.

The root cause of constant manipulation is often deep-seated and complex. It is not easy to deal with an individual who is psychologically manipulative irrespective of the reasons why he is the way he is. Being on the receiving end of manipulative aggression is never pleasant. Learning to deal with psychological manipulation is the best way to protect yourself from emotional abuse. You will learn about the simple ways in which you can handle manipulative people.

Dealing with Manipulators

You can come across manipulators in all aspects of your life, both professional and personal. Whether you want to believe it or not, even those you love the most and hold dear can be manipulators. You might have to deal with manipulative partners, manipulative parents, or even manipulative coworkers. Regardless of the manipulator, you are dealing with. It isn't always easy, but you must learn to do so. After all, you are the only one who is responsible for your overall wellbeing.

Basic Fundamental Rights

A fundamental right is inalienable, and no one can take it away from you. This is one thing you must keep in mind whenever you come across any person who is a psychological manipulator. You must not only recognize your rights but must also prevent the violation of these rights. As long as you don't harm others, you must stand up for yourself and protect your rights at all costs. If you knowingly harm someone, you may lose some of these fundamental rights. Here are a couple of basic human rights you must be aware of.

- You have the right to be treated with dignity and respect.

- You are free to express your opinions, feelings, desires, and wants.

- You are free to set your priorities, and no one can force you to do something.

- You don't have to feel guilty when you say "no."

- You have the right to set specific boundaries for yourself.

- You have the right to have different opinions, and you don't have to agree with everyone.

- You not only have a right, but an obligation to safeguard yourself mentally, emotionally, and physically.

All these fundamental rights define your boundaries. You must not only enforce your limitations on others but must also respect them yourself. Of course, you'll come across people who don't respect your rights. Especially those who resort to psychological manipulation, strive to deprive others of their rights so that they can exert control over you. However, keep in mind, you have the power to decide what you want to do, and you are the only one in charge of your life.

Maintain Some Distance

A manipulator often puts up a façade for the world to see and doesn't let his true intentions rise to the surface. A simple way to detect or spot a manipulator is to see the way he acts in front of different people and various situations. Most of us tend to exhibit social differentiation to a certain degree; emotional predators and psychological manipulators tend to dwell on the extreme ends of the spectrum. An emotional manipulator can be extremely polite one instant and unnervingly hostile the next. If you notice this kind of behavior from anyone in your circle, maintain your distance. If you cannot get away from such a person or avoid social interactions, then limit your interactions. Spend as little time dealing with such a person as possible. Even being around them will hurt you in ways you cannot begin to comprehend. You don't have to worry about being responsible for their feelings. If the manipulator tries to make you feel guilty for maintaining your distance, it is a part of his manipulative nature, and you're not obligated to fix them. So, stay away.

No Personalization

A manipulator is continuously going to look for your weaknesses, and once he understands them, he will exploit them. Therefore, he might try to make you feel inadequate, doubt your sanity, and question your judgment. If you experience any of these feelings, then it means the manipulator has a stronghold over you. Don't ever blame yourself in such situations because it only increases the power the manipulator has. In such instances, remind yourself, you are not the problem, and there is nothing wrong with you. Take a moment to think about the relationship you share with the manipulator and answer the following questions.

- Does this person seem to have unreasonable demands and expectations from me?

- Does he treat me with the respect I deserve?

- Is this relationship well-balanced, or does it only favor him?

- Does this relationship make me feel good about myself?

If your answer is in the affirmative, then there is nothing wrong with the relationship. However, if it isn't, then you are in a relationship with a manipulator. Your answers to these questions will give insight into the kind of person you're dealing with. So, stop blaming yourself, and instead look at the other person.

Probing Questions

A psychological manipulator will inevitably start making requests. These requests are subtly veiled demands. Often the claims made will be such that you are required to go out of your way to meet his needs. If the claim you're presented with seems to be unreasonable, it's time to shift the attention back onto the manipulator by asking a couple of questions. By doing this, you can judge for yourself whether the person has sufficient self-awareness to realize the unreasonableness of his demands. Here are a couple of probing questions you can ask.

- Is this a request or a demand?

- What will I get if I fulfill this?

- Does this sound fair to you?

- Does this seem reasonable?

- Do you expect me to (restate the demand) do this?

By asking such probing questions, you are placing a mirror in front of the manipulator to check his true nature and intentions. If the manipulator has even a little self-awareness, he will quickly withdraw his demand or even apologize for it. However, it is quite unlikely that an emotional predator will have any awareness about the unreasonableness of his request and might expect you to comply regardless. If the manipulator tries to turn the tables on you and say you are overreacting or are being unreasonable, steer clear of him. Either way, you have your answer.

Time Is Your Ally

Not only will the manipulator make unreasonable demands but will also expect an immediate answer. By doing this, he is trying to maximize the stress placed on you to exert a higher degree of control over you and on the situation. In such instances, don't play right into the manipulator's trap and buy yourself some time. A suitable response is, "I will get back to you later," or "I will need to think about it." If you don't respond to this demand immediately, you are preventing him from controlling you. Once you have sufficient time, and can carefully analyze the situation along with its pros and cons. If you feel like it is an unreasonable demand, then you have the right to say "no."

Saying "NO"

A lot of people often struggle with saying "no." You must not only be firm while declining a request but must also do it diplomatically. After all, you do want to prevent the manipulator from creating an unnecessary scene, don't you? You have the right to say "no," and don't let anyone take this away from you. If you allow someone else to control your actions like a puppeteer, you are giving away your power to choose. You can say "no" whenever you want to, and you don't have to feel guilty about it. Don't let the manipulator shame you or make you feel guilty for not complying with his demands.

Confrontation

An emotional predator, like a manipulator or a narcissist, is essentially a bully. While dealing with a bully, keep in mind that they are often targeting those whom they perceive to be weak or soft targets. As long as you don't take any action, stay compliant, and passive, the bully will always have some control over you. A lot of bullies put up a facade of courage and are often cowardly on the inside. So, once a target starts disobeying them or not complying with their request, bullies tend to back down. This stands right not just for a bully in school, but also in a personal or professional environment. If you ever decide to confront a bully, ensure that you are in a safe and secure environment. Make sure the bully cannot harm you and if required, opt for public confrontations. Having a couple of witnesses around you will be quite helpful. If you need help, ask for it and don't try to do everything by yourself.

Importance of Consequences

You must not only establish certain boundaries but must also set consequences for the violation of those boundaries. Whenever you feel like someone is violating your limitations, you must deploy a result. This is an important skill, especially while dealing with tricky and unscrupulous individuals.

At times, regardless of all that you do, being around a manipulator can cause irreparable damage to your overall wellbeing. In such instances, you might have to sever all ties and run in the opposite direction. If that's what you need to do for your wellbeing, then don't hesitate. You owe it to yourself, and you deserve better than being manipulated. So, don't sell yourself short and don't subject yourself to manipulative abuse.

CHAPTER - 4

ART OF PERSUASION

Being influential and persuasive is a skill that you can actually develop. With the right tips and knowledge, you can master the art of influence and persuasion and apply it is in various aspects of your life. If you are an entrepreneur or someone who's daily routine needs to convince others to see things based on your own perspectives and get them to agree with you, then mastering persuasion is an advantage. You need to hone this type of personality from the time you have chosen your own career.

With excellent persuasion skills, it will be easier for you to present your new ideas to the public. You can persuade the correct partners to be part of your network, create and present solutions to the right people, convince potential investors to fund your ideas, and convince customers to buy from you.

The good news is that you can have this skill.

Here are just some ways for you to master the art of persuasion:

Practice Repetition

Repetition is an effective way for you to get the attention of people. A lot of people, especially entrepreneurs, make the wrong assumption that their passion in their chosen field is enough to help them clearly send their message to the right audience and stand out from the crowd. This is a wrong assumption because with the excessive amount of information that the public can access from various sources, it would be difficult for you to stand out. In fact, the majority of the public today already created filters as a means of ignoring unsolicited inputs.

You can combat this by ensuring that you practice repetition. Note that you will most likely convince the public that your message is worthy to be heard if they see and hear it many times – both in verbal and written form. The good news is that with this repetition, you can also imbibe the skill of persuasion into your own personality, especially because it aids you in mastering it.

Use Imagination

Another way to master the art of persuasion is to use your own and your target audience's imagination. For instance, you can say things like "can you imagine how happy you'll feel by buying this product?". This will give your audience the opportunity to pain a clear picture of what he/she can expect to receive if he agrees on what you are saying or take what you are offering. Let him/her imagine the pleasure of following what you are suggesting, and the pain that he/she will most likely feel if he/she does not.

Try to Obtain A Yes Early

If you are an entrepreneur, for instance, then try to persuade your target audience to agree with you, even in just trivial matters. It could be as simple as the weather, whether the color of an object is blue, politics, etc. Keep in mind that getting someone to like you is one of the most important aspects of persuasion. It would be possible for you to reach that goal if the person you are dealing with agrees with you.

If you are still a beginner in the art of persuasion, then try to let your target audience clearly see the actual value of what you're offering. You should also clearly indicate what they will be missing if they decide not to have it. Take advantage of the power of leading questions, like "do you want to", "have you been wanting to", etc.

The questions should be leading enough that they will have a difficult time saying no to. You need to customize the questions to ensure that they suit the type of conversation you're having with your audience to persuade them to agree with you at the earliest possible time.

Build Your Confidence

You can't expect to master the art of persuasion if you're not confident. Your audience should see how confident you are with what you're saying. How can you expect someone to believe in what you're saying if you, yourself, have doubts about it? No matter how competent you are, if your target audience does not sense your confidence, then you'll most likely lose the fight and be left unable to convince them.

When it comes to building your persuasion skills, note that you can develop your confidence by fully understanding how important it is to facilitate a need. Keep in mind that many people need your help and you hold the answers to a certain problem they are facing. Believe that what you're offering or saying is important and can provide a solution to a problem – that is regardless of the field you're in – whether you're in web design, foods, etc.

Keep in mind that someone will always find your products, services and solutions helpful. Believing that you have something that is of great value to someone can significantly increase your confidence, thereby making it easier for you to convince/persuade someone.

Improve Your Listening Skills

The ability to listen to someone intently – whether it's your customers, friends, colleagues, starting entrepreneurs, small business owners, or industry experts – contributes a lot to successfully persuading someone. Through intent listening, you will learn a lot more about the field you're in. Try to listen more than speak. Note that the time you spent not speaking are frequently the most vital moments since the other party will most likely feel that you are genuinely valuing his time.

Listening is also known to be one of the keys to being persuasive. In a study conducted in a business school in Columbia, for instance, researchers discovered that a lot of workers value listening skills too much that this lead to the successful implementation of persuasion. With the set of experiments and tests they conducted, they were able to find out that one's ability to persuade or influence has a huge relationship to the timing he chooses to be verbal when doing the act. Remember that even if you do not speak and just merely listen, you can still persuade others using body language and cues.

Learn How To Integrate Connection In All Your Persuasion Endeavors

Regardless of whom you are trying to influence/persuade, forging a connection is crucial. Keep in mind that as humans, there is a great likelihood for them to respond positively if you use emotional appeals by connecting to them. The great philosopher, Aristotle, for instance, discovered that it is greatly possible for humans to be influenced if one uses a mix of credible, logically argumentative and emotional appeals. Using emotional appeals more also increases the number of people who can be persuaded.

If you are an entrepreneur who needs to persuade people most of the time, then you can also use and mirror that concept to your advantage. A wise tip is to connect to them in a more emotional level by matching your voice inflections, physical cues and charisma. This is a huge help in building an emotional connection, thereby allowing the person you're talking to realize that you also have similarities. This will eventually forge a bond of trust.

Learn How To Give Praises

You also need to learn the art of giving praise when it comes to developing your persuasion skills. If you just focus on shooting people with your ideas without even listening to them or making them feel that you also value them, they will feel like they are insignificant. This will cause them to focus on mending their hurt egos, instead of listening intently to what you have today. The good news is that you can be more likable to them if you start to offer them praise. Find something good about the person you're talking to and praise him.

Once he finds you likable through the praises that you give, it will be easier for you to persuade him to listen to you and agree with your idea. Praising someone can make him feel like he is attaining his personal achievement. He will then like you more and he will start thinking that you will be of great help to him when it comes to reaching his full potential.

Just make sure that you're careful when offering praises, though. Avoid resorting to using empty praises. Doing so will only damage your efforts.

CHAPTER - 5

DARK PSYCHOLOGY

At its root, dark psychology is all about mind control. You can influence what other people think or do by understanding the inner workings of the other person's mind. You can persuade them into behaving in certain ways, making them feel as though what they have done is of their own volition even though you were behind the scenes, orchestrating the actions the entire time. You can motivate people to help you by helping them first. You know that they are more likely to offer help if you help them first simply because people tend to reciprocate. When you understand how the minds of those around you work, you can begin utilizing it to your advantage.

Dark psychology refers to the ability to manipulate and control the minds of others. It typically entails both manipulation and coercion. In the wrong hands, it can be devastating, but understanding what it is can be the difference between being manipulated as a target yourself and being able to use the concepts within dark psychology without falling victim to the darkness at its core. You can use the ideas without being evil or malicious, though there is quite a fine line between using it ethically and falling into the darkness.

We are indeed human at the end of the day. It is because of this very reason that we get to dwell allot on the opinion of others in everything that we do. We always desire and adore getting validation from others so that we can subconsciously decide whether or not we shall be depressed. In this age of the millennial, the norm has become to just brag about their wealth on social media. A lot of these bragging are often than not the truth. This ultimately leads to one having a loose relationship with reality. Self-deception of this type can dig deep into the human spicy, that a victim of these may one day wake up and realize that their perfect world is only existent within their maids. Depression will closely follow suit.

The first step to attempting to defend yourself from Dark Psychology is confronting the situation and taking the stance of breaking off any illusions you may have. You will not be able to proceed normally with your life. You have to be wary of the fact that you are in control of your own choices. Then make the conscious choice of seeing things for what they are. That deal, which seems too good to be true, could actually be just that... too good to be true. The other thing you should follow is to definitely trust your instincts.

The truth is that our self-disappointment can make us choose the answers we receive. We tell ourselves that we listen, but we only pay attention to the answers we want to hear rather than to the answers we receive. You may have broken the illusions around you, but some of you are still clinging to the comfort of those illusions. The pain of confronting the situation would prevent you from listening to the real answers to your questions.

Actual listening requires a certain sense of detachment, but this time around not from reality. You have to get rid of your emotions. Your detachment from our emotions would lead you to the next step, which would logically process the new information. It can complicate situations more than they already are to act irrationally. It makes your exit strategy so much difficult to let all the emotions simmer and spring to the surface.

When you face the truth, the irrational part of you may want you to let it all go hell. Your rightly justified anger can inspire you to take steps to calm your emotions in the short term. But you may come to regret these actions in the long term. I'm not saying that you should deny your emotions; I'm not saying that you do not act on these emotions.

Act Quickly

It's great that you have come to terms with the reality of things. But defense against these dark manipulative tactics entail so much more. While attempting to defend you from the claws of these manipulators, is often intense and exhilarating at first. This intensity of these emotions may cause one to slowly slide into denial. The more you delay in taking any action is usually what accelerates the onset of this denial, and when it happens, there are high chances that you might relapse and end up getting trapped in the same web. This can be avoided by taking action immediately you realize that someone is trying to manipulate you. This can present itself in the simplest of ways like when informing a close friend of some reality of the particular situation may be all that's needed so set in motion a series of events that will eventually lead to your freedom.

You should know that the fabric of illusion is made from tougher material than glass after making the choice to act. The illusion could work its way back into your heart with your emotions in high gear by using fragments of your emotions to fix it. When a liar is caught in a lie, he or she may attempt to recruit others to enforce that lie when they feel that they are no longer holding you. A deceptive partner with whom you have recently broken things off would at this point try to use the other mutual relationships in your life to change your mind. If you want to get out of this unscathed, you will need both your logic and instincts.

Although the truth of the situation is that when you discover that you've been lied to consistently, you become emotionally scarred, so the issue of leaving the situation unscathed becomes silent. Priority should be given, however, to take the route that allows you to leave this toxic situation without harming yourself further. You're all over the place emotionally. Rage, anger, hurt, and deception is the iceberg's tip. But logically, you need to think. Keep your head above the water and warn yourself.

Get Help Fast

When you're trapped by other people's manipulations, confusion is one of the emotions you'd experience. This helps cloud your rational thinking and leaves you feeling helpless. You might even question the reality of what you are facing at this point. It would lead to denial if you continue to entertain these doubts.

Similarly, getting another person's opinion can help you discern the truth of the situation and what might be your next steps. Just remember, it's better to go to someone who has proved countless times they're interested in your best. The next step is to confront the perpetrator if you have the help you need. For this, I suggest you choose the scene or location. Choose a place you know that gives you the upper hand. On your part, that would require some careful planning. If the perpetrator exists in the cyber world, especially if the person swindled you of your money, you would have to involve the police and the relevant authorities. Do some of your own investigations so as to ascertain the truth. After you face the perpetrator and take the necessary steps to get out of the situation, you must start the healing process quickly.

The scale and gravity to which you were hurt, manipulated or abused do not matter. You must be able to walk past it and wait until you can "heal" your wounds, rather than sitting on your couch and reliving the past. Time would give you enough distance from your experience. If you don't do anything about it, an unhealthy scab could form over the wound, which would make you as vulnerable if not more than you had experienced. Speak to a counselor, attend therapy, and take an active part in facilitating the healing process, whatever you choose to do. It won't happen overnight, but you are sure that you get closer to improving every day and every step you take in therapy.

Trust Your Instincts

While your brain interprets signals based on facts, logic, and sometimes experience, your heart works in the opposite direction by screening information through an emotional filter. The only thing that picks up vibrations is your gut instinct, which neither the heart nor the brain can pick on. And if you can groom to the point where you recognize your inner voice and are trained to react to it, you will lower your chances of being seduced by people trying to work on you with their manipulative will. To begin with, it's hard to recognize this voice. And that's because we allowed voices of doubt, self-discrimination as well as the critics ' loud voices within and without drowning out our authentic voice over the course of our lives. Your survival depends on this voice or instinct. So, trust that when it kicks in, your brain neurons can still process things in your immediate vicinity.

Some people call it intuition, and some refer to it as instinct, especially when it comes to relationships, they are undoubtedly the same thing. You must accept that it may not always make logical sense to start trusting your instincts. If you've ever been in the middle of doing something and experienced the feeling of being watched all of a sudden, then you know what I mean. You don't have eyes at the back of your head, there's no one else with you in the room, but you get the tiny shiver running down your spine and the "sudden knowledge" you're watching. That's what I'm talking about. The first step to connect with your instinct is to decode your mind with the voices you've let in. With meditation, you can do this. Forget the chatter of "he said, she said." Concentrate on your center. You are the voice you know. Next, be careful about your thoughts. Don't just throw away the eclectic monologs in your head. Rather go with the thoughts flow.

Why do you think of a certain person in some way? How do you feel so deeply about this person, even if you only knew each other for a few days? What's that nagging feeling about this other person that you have? You get more tuned to your intuition as you explore your thoughts and understand when your instincts kick and how to react to it. You may need to learn to take a step back to pause and think if you are the kind of person who prefers to make spur decisions at the moment. This moment in which you pause gives you the opportunity to really reflect on your decisions and evaluate them. The next part is a hard part and it couldn't be followed by many people. Unfortunately, you can't skip or navigate around this step. This part has to do with trust. You need to be open to the idea of trusting yourself and trusting others to be able to trust your instinct. Your failure to trust others would just make you paranoid, and it's not your instincts that kick when you're paranoid.

It's the fear of you. Fear tends to turn every molehill into a hill. You must let go of your fear, embrace confidence, and let that lead in your new relationships.

CHAPTER - 6

BODY LANGUAGE

Body language points to the nonverbal cues that us as humans use to have effective communication with each other. Such nonverbal signals, according to scholars, constitute a major part of daily interaction. The stuff we do not say can still transmit amounts of knowledge from our body language to our physical movements. It has also been reported that body language can account for about 60 percent and 65 percent of all communication. It is necessary to understand body language, and it is also vital to pay close attention to other signals such as meaning. In many situations, instead of relying on a single event, you must look at signals as a band. When you learn and master how to use body language for effective communication, you will also be able to manipulate individuals psychologically in a positive manner.

What Is Body Language?

Even when they don't express their opinions verbally, the majority still miss clues about what they think and feel. Non-verbal signals communicated through the formation of the sender's body, physical appearance, voice inflections and intensity of the voice, and various signs are all referred to as non-verbal communication.

Non-verbal communication is usually not as simple as it is conveyed in words, but how it is expressed could take on a major job by recognizing somebody and interfacing with others. It's a quiet ensemble: mini-expressions (short presentations of feeling that individual attempts to disguise), hand gestures, and the recording of posture in the human mind very rapidly in any event, when someone is not consciously aware of them.

These acknowledgment snapshots, however short, can have lasting repercussions on how an individual translates the inspiration, disposition, and receptivity of others as well as how they see their own inner identity. Regrettably, certain psychological well-being issues, particularly neuropsychiatric issues such as mental defect, may make it, even more, trying to test to recognize and respond to non-verbal communication messages.

Types of Body Language

There are types of body language. This is because we cannot classify the different styles in the same category. Different body languages can be distinguished. So, which body language styles can be differentiated? Generally, the body language is divided into two columns. That includes; Body parts and the Intent

So what kinds in each class can be observed?

Let us start with the body parts and the language they communicate.

- The Head - The placement of the head and its movement, back and forth, right to left, side to side, including the shake of hair.

- Face - This includes facial expressions. You should note that the face has many muscles ranging from 54 and 98 whose work is to move different areas of the face. The movements of the face depict the state of your mind.

- Eyebrows - The eyebrows can express themselves through moving up and down, as well as giving a frown

- Eyes - The eyes can be rolled, move up down, right, and left, blink as well as the dilatation

- The Nose - The expression of the nose can be by the flaring of the nostrils and the formation of wrinkles at the top

- The Lips - There are many roles played by the lips, that include snarling, smiling, kissing, opened, closed, tight, and puckering

- The Tongue - The tongue can roll in and out, go up and down, touch while kissing, and also the licking of lips

- The Jaw - The jaw opens and closes, it can be clinched and also the lower jaw can be moved right and left

- Your Body Posture - This describes the way you place your body, legs, and arms connected, and also concerning other people

- The Body Proximity - This looks at how far your body is to other people

- Shoulder Movements - They move up and down, get hunched, and hang

- The Arm - These go up down, straight and crossed

Legs and the feet-these can have an expression in many different ways. They can be straight, crossed, legs placed one over the other, the feet can face the next person you are in a conversation with, they can face away from each other, the feet can be dangling the shoes

The hand and the fingers-the way that your

hands and fingers move is powerful in reading other people's gestures. The hands can move up and down, they can do some hidden language that only people of the same group can understand.

How one reacts to handling and placing of objects-this is not regarded as a body part but it technically plays a role in reading a body language. This may predict anger, happiness and much more.

This includes willingly making body movements otherwise known as gestures. These are the movements that you intended to make for example shaking of hands, blinking your eyes, moving, and shaking your body in a sexy way maybe to lure someone and much more. There are also involuntary movements-this are movements that you have no control over. This can be sweating, laughter, crying and much more.

Importance of Body Language

Most individuals rely on social networks and texts to connect in the modern digital age, and this is a very reliable way for doing so.

While digital communication enables people to speak at convenience and can reduce stress on certain individuals, something can be lost in so doing, and because you are incapable of recognizing the person when you speak to them, you can miss key non-verbal signs in addition to verbal ones such as vocal inflections. Digital communication has become the main method for people around the world, and to satisfy this, there is the likelihood that body language will proceed to develop. Most of the time you may hear the negatives of body language. Maybe you are told not to twist in a certain way, sit this way or that way. However, body language can influence your life positively. Let us look at what you should do to maximize body language.

How Body Language Can Influence Effective Communication

While we may feel and wish that interaction is as easy as the phrases that we say, it is not the truth. The reality is that our message is heard more than just our words. If in an email, text, or instant message you've ever been mistaken, you know what I'm talking about. Words alone are not enough. The body language is part of what strengthens and wraps up the message and if individuals see us may be face-to-face or using video cameras, our body language influences our message and presentation. You may find that body language helps the receiver of information read your mind and interpret your thoughts. Acknowledge that there's more to the message that you're sending, there's the meta-message of who you're and the intention to send that message. Body language is constantly communicating to your audience.

My aim in this is to offer you some specific advice to help your communication in the body language that you use and to increase the chances that your message will be heard and understood properly.

The Power of The Outstretched Hand

It is the source of some of the most powerful body signals, whether in the transmission of commands or commands or in a simple handshake. The open hand, if properly displayed, gives the executor of the gesture unquestionable authority. Remember that the pointed index finger raises negative feelings in most listeners.

The Secret of Laughter and Smiles - The Gestures Are Fantastic

Scientists are able to distinguish true smiles from false ones using the so-called FACS.

True smiles are unconsciously generated by the brain, which means that they are automatic. When you feel pleasure, some signs circulate through the part of your brain that processes emotion, causing the muscles of your mouth to move, your cheeks rise, your eyes narrow and your eyebrows droop slightly.

Have you ever heard of "mirror neurons"? What is most remarkable is that smiling at a person provokes a reciprocal and equal reaction, even when both smiles are false.

Attention to Signs with Arms

There are countless signs. Here we will remember that crossing your arms appreciably diminishes your credibility. It means putting a barrier between you and the other person. A strong message: "I am not willing, I do not accept, I do not go, etc. ..."

So, crossing your arms in front of your body is always seen as negative, and the message is both in the head of the recipient and in the person, who sends it. Even if you fold your arms because, say, you have back pain, the observer will unconsciously perceive you as a closed person to your ideas.

Signs by Look

It's like magic. How many times have you heard that the "eyes are the mirror of the soul"? What the pupils want to tell us. Reading through the gestures of the pupils.

The pupils bring very subtle messages, which often go unnoticed. However, they have their own language that can be deciphered. The most visible aspect is the dilation of the pupils, which automatically changes size according to the circumstances and without our intervention.

Usually, the pupils dilate when we see an interesting object and that we accept without hesitation, or in the penumbra when we have difficulty to see something. If lighting and visibility conditions are normal, dilation of the pupil is a sign of interest and attraction.

The opposite is also true. When we are faced with something we reject or feel afraid, the pupil's contract. The contracted pupils show hostility or bad mood, even if we are not looking directly at the object that displeases us.

The eyes move. They tell us a lot. Watch the movements. The movement of the eyes is continuous. Waking up or sleeping, there is always a movement. Something we can read / capture.

When the eyes move upward and lean to the right, the person is trying to imagine, describing, creativity.

If the movement is up and to the left, we activate the functions related to memories.

Looking down and to the right, we remember a feeling.

Now look down and to the left, we are talking to ourselves.

Small Examples of Non-Verbal Communication

Pay attention, study more, look for information. It is a subject that requires dedication, however, once you master it is very interesting.

Closed Eyes

It is more than likely that a person who keeps his eyes closed during a conversation wishes to protect himself from the world. It is important to note that this is not a sign of fear. Instead, it is an attempt to ward off an unwanted presence or thought. When the eyes are closed, you cannot see things around you, including you.

Hands on Your Mouth

You probably remember that reference in children. Children put their hands over their mouths when they do not want to talk about anything. Adults do it sometimes, too. A palm or fist over the mouth restricts the flow of words.

This action may also manifest in the form of a cough or sneezing.

Biting Your Glasses

A person who bites his glasses may need a little joy. That someone is probably worried about something. Biting things is a subconscious manifestation of the need to feel secure.

Face Projection

Physical gestures that call attention to the face are more often reserved for members of the opposite sex. A man who recognizes this body language would know that that is a great time to praise a woman about her appearance.

Rubbing the Chin

This usually happens when a person is making a decision. The eyes may be focused on an object or wandering in various directions. This is because the individual is probably thinking deeply and is not aware of what is happening around them.

CHAPTER - 7

PROXEMICS

Now, imagine that you are standing in front of someone. You can see that they are crossing their arms with hands hidden behind them, their eyes shifting nervously from you to veer off to the left every now and then. They shift their weight from foot to foot and struggle to maintain eye contact. Something about the body language of this person makes you uneasy, but you cannot place it. They are keeping their distance from you, and every time you approach closer, you notice that they are likely to move away.

Body language is good at giving us feelings that tell us to be on edge, offended, or relaxed, but if you do not know what you are reading, you are going to struggle to understand why you are feeling that way. It can be difficult to know what someone intends if you cannot put meaning to what they are doing. You can have a general idea of how you want to respond, but it can be incredibly beneficial

Proxemics refers to the distance between yourself and someone else—it is the usage of space between yourself and the world around you. Naturally, people put varying degrees of space between themselves and others, and when you are looking to understand proxemics, the best way to do so is to consider it a judgment of the relationship between yourself and those around you. You can also judge the relationships of others based upon the distance they put between each other, both vertical and horizontal.

The Use Of Vertical Space

Vertical space is exactly what it sounds like—it is the space relative to your own position height-wise. When someone is utilizing vertical space, they are attempting to make themselves taller or shorter, depending on the context. Those who want to make themselves taller may want to be seen as an authority or otherwise as someone that is deserving of respect and compliance. They may even use this space when they are trying to look at others who are taller than them—they simply tilt their heads back to look down their nose at the taller person to create the same impact.

When you make yourself smaller, you typically want to be seen as less dominant for some reason. You may be attempting to shrink down to speak to a child in order to truly be understood, for example, or you may be lowering yourself to make yourself seem more submissive. In particular, people will pull their chins inward when they want to be seen as smaller because they will then be required to look up through their eyelashes at the other person, even if the other person is taller.

The default, eye level, is deemed to be the most respectful—it marks you and the other person as equals deserving of the same respect and consideration.

The Use Of Horizontal Space

In horizontal space, you are looking at how near or far people are to each other. You will use this when you are picking apart the relationships of others. In particular, there are four distances that are used between each other, ranging from intimate distances all the way to the public distance.

- The intimate distance: This refers to being as close as possible to the other person. When you are in this position, you are usually touching without trying, or close enough to do so. This is typically for young children and parents, or for lovers that are comfortable being this close to each other. Generally speaking, this zone is only about 18 inches away from you.

- The personal distance: Slightly further away than the intimate distance, the personal distance covers about 18 inches away up to about 5 feet around you. This is what people are talking about when they say that you are invading their personal bubbles. This zone is usually reserved for those that you like or feel comfortable with, such as friends and family members, or children that are too old to be within the intimate zone. The closer you can get to the center, the closer your relationship with that other person.

- The social distance: This is a bit further out. This is the distance that you naturally try to maintain with strangers around you, or when you are interacting with someone else that you do not know. Typically, this is between about 5 and 10 feet. You will use this when you are out and about unless you have no choice otherwise. When you are forced to encroach on this distance, most often, you will make it a point to ignore the other person in an attempt to ignore the fact that they are violating those personal boundaries, such as if you are sitting on the bus.

- The public distance: This is even further out— this refers to anything beyond about 12 feet and is reserved for instances in which you are speaking out toward a crowd. You want to be loud enough that everyone in the crowd can speak, so you want to ensure that people are a bit further away from you so they can see and hear you easier. This is reserved for lectures in classrooms, for example, or in performances.

CHAPTER - 8

HOW TO ANALYZE

PEOPLE

In psychology, analyzing people means using people's statements, studying their behaviors, and their actions to make assumptions about what is going on in their mind or what they think about. This is something humans often do when they are interacting with one another. It's entirely natural to read other people's minds and analyze them. Contrary to this, a lot of people think that psychology is magic that people use to enter other people's minds to determine their thinking and ultimately manipulate them. However, this is not the case. Anyone can read other people's minds if you are observant and you pay attention to their actions and behavior.

You don't have to be a psychologist to manipulate people; moreover, having the psychological understanding to know how people think and how this process influences their behavior does not give you the automatic capability to manipulate them. The primary focus of analyzing people is to understand how they think and why they think that way. This information can be shared with the individuals and the society for improvements where necessary.

Reasons for Analyzing People

Word cues cannot give full coverage of someone's personality traits, though they provide a deep understanding of somebody's thoughts and the character of his behavior. This means that assumptions can be formulated and can be tested using additional information from third-party collaboration. The human mind is incredibly smart and efficient. We only use the nouns and the verbs when we speak, and other parts of speech are added afterward during the transformation of ideas into spoken language.

Analyzing people enables the observers to make assumptions about their behaviors. For example, if you observe a person who is always timely, you might conclude that this is a person that strictly obeys the social norms and lives according to the expectations of those who rely on him.

Some people can also argue that individuals

with this kind of behavioral characteristic can make a good employee because he or she is committed to his work and does not want to disappoint the employers. Ultimately, analyzing people is a noninvasive technique that allows you to obtain information and make a conclusion about people without them knowing.

Techniques of Analyzing People

In fields such as social work and psychology, the work of a psychiatrist is to analyze people not only by what they say but who they are in general. Interpreting both the verbal and nonverbal cues used by a person, psychiatrists seek to understand the true nature of a person. If you choose to employ logic alone, it won't give you the whole picture of that person. You must apply other crucial forms of obtaining information so that you will be placed in a suitable position that you can read various nonverbal cues given off by people. You must also be willing to surrender preoccupation with factors such as ego or emotional crushes that can hinder you from seeing a person clearly. You need to be objective and central to receive the information neutrally without any interference.

It doesn't matter on the person that you are analyzing, because to understand people fully, you must avoid biases. The three techniques that are involved in analyzing people include:

Listen to Your Intuition

Intuition can be said to be what your gut feeling tells you and not what your mind tells you. It is a kind of nonverbal information that is mainly perceived via images and the body instead of concentrating on the logic. If you want to understand somebody better, what matters most is who the person is. Having a strong intuition will help you to see more than the obvious to reveal the reality under other physical aspects. You need to honor your gut feelings especially when you see that particular person for the first time before you have a chance to reconsider your assumptions. Gut feelings occur quickly, and you don't have the time to weigh your options. This is the body's internal truth meter which tells you whether you should trust people.

You must be aware of goosebumps; these are intuitive tingles that alert us to the connection of the people who move to inspire us. It also occurs whereby you experience a feeling as you have ever met a person before. Goosebumps are the body's instinctive tool to alert you. You also need to pay attention to insight flashes. In a conversation, you can get a sentiment about people, and though it might be negative, you need to remain positive and focused.

In some cases, you might experience a situation whereby you feel other people's physical symptoms and emotions in yourself. For this reason, you ought to watch your intuitive empathy to ensure that you remain on the right course.

Have you anytime looked at someone and thought you had them understood just from that look? Is it exact to state that you were right? Or then again would you say you were stirred up about some piece of their character? Despite whether you were right or wrong, you essentially tried getting someone, which is an ability that most of us would love to have. Everything considered, in case you can tell when your chief is feeling incredible, you understand when to demand a raise, right? When you understand your people are feeling awful you know, it is anything but a chance to tell them you scratched their vehicle. It is connected to appreciating what understanding people means and how it capacities.

What Is Reading People'?

When you look at someone and feel like you can condemn whether they are feeling extraordinary or a horrendous one, paying little heed to whether they are a wonderful individual or a mean one or whatever else using any and all means, you are getting them. At the point when all is said in done, understanding someone means researching them and it does not just should be a speedy look, and knowing something about them without them saying anything in any way shape or form. It is a tendency you get from looking and from viewing the way in which they stand, the way wherein they look around, the way where they move. There some different features that could play into your inclination and cognizance of them, yet the most critical thing is that they did not explicitly uncover to you whatever that thing is.

Understanding people can empower you to acknowledge who to approach with that unprecedented new idea (and when to approach) and who you ought to stay away from. It, in like manner, discloses to you how to familiarize something with them, paying little mind to whether from a precise perspective or dynamically fun and creative one. Before you know it, understanding people will be normal to you if you practice it routinely enough. Additionally, what's shockingly better is that you have no doubt been doing it for as long as you can remember and not despite contemplating it. That is in light of the fact that it is something that even kids will give a shot every so often, without acknowledging how huge it is.

Understanding People in Childhood

When you were an adolescent did you ever sit on a seat at the entertainment focus or on your porch and watch people walk around? You apparently did at some point or another, paying little mind to whether it was uniquely for a few minutes. Also, a short time later you look at the overall public and make stories. In the occasion that they're walking a canine, perhaps they're a pooch walker on their way to the entertainment focus. In the occasion that they're passing on an organizer case and walking quickly, they are late to a noteworthy social affair, clearly, that get-together may have been with outcasts in your young character, anyway, you get a general idea. You have successfully deciphered what you see of someone to make a story about them.

Getting Help Reading People

Understanding people is a noteworthy ability to learn. For a large number of individuals, you probably look at is an 'acknowledge the main decision accessible' circumstance, is not that so? You accept on the off chance that I can scrutinize people, at that point extraordinary, yet if I cannot, well, no harm was done, is that not so? Everything considered, understanding people energizes you a lot in your life and it causes you to be a prevalent individual as well, which is the reason it is a critical ability to have, paying little respect to whether you have a straightforward appreciation or an undeniably expansive one.

Starting with People You Know

It will, in general, be less complex to start scrutinizing the all-inclusive community you know before continuing forward to untouchables. These are people that you certainly know things about, and when you look at them, you can in all probability watch things that show those qualities. If your nearest friend is excessively bubbly and pleasant to everyone, you can undoubtedly look at them and jump on that trademark. Venture up to the plate and see them, see what it is about them that shows others they are bubbly and all around arranged and a while later quest for those characteristics in different people around you.

Research is Showing this to be True

Various people with mind hurts, oftentimes to the frontal folds of the cerebrum, develop excessively poor social aptitudes and social direct regardless of modestly incredible insight.

People with mental unevenness range issue seem to experience extraordinary difficulty with social information. From a transformative perspective, it looks good that social discernment may have developed freely to non-social aptitudes.

More Imitation

Inside the mind itself, "reflect" neuron systems in the premotor cortex of the frontal projection are started when we watch the exercises of others. It creates the impression that we do not just reflect considerations, we furthermore reflect exercises!

Right when sound adults are set in fMRI scanners and got some data about the mental state of someone such as themselves, a comparative region of the prefrontal cortex is impelled as when they think about themselves. This additionally means we appreciate others by reference to ourselves.

CHAPTER - 9

USING BODY LANGUAGE

One of the most important things to remember is that others see you as you see yourself: enhancing your mood by positive body language is the key ingredient to good communication. Nonetheless, there are ways we can be mindful when it comes to using our bodies to communicate.

Conversation / Rapport

Building a bond with a new person or establishing ties with old friends is the most important part of building a good relationship. It is something in body language circles that is talked about a lot because it is the main goal of most experiences. When you are in a good relationship, you are going to respond well to the body language of the other person, and you are going to want to be with each other instantly, whether it is in a professional or personal capacity. So how do you build a relationship without a natural spark or common ground? You do this with a body language style known as mirroring and matching.

Mirroring and matching is quite literally what it sounds like: you mimic another person's body language so you can create a connection right away and make it simple. People tend to like a similar wavelength and familiar attitude, spending time with others; this will be created by keeping the bodies in harmony. You need to look at how an individual behaves and acts to do this, are they closed? Open? Should they talk quickly or slowly? What are the styles of hand gestures they use? Seek even to see how easily they breathe and what kind of personal body space they prefer. Then you can try to copy it. You shouldn't try to mimic some kind of Groucho Marx, but just take a similar pose naturally, so you are as comfortable or on the edge as they are; if they use big arm motions, then try to do the same thing. Do try to match the pace and tone they speak, do not try to match their accent, but stop using fancy words if they do not use them. For example, if the other party is using the word fascinating, do not start using marvelous to explain the same thing, just use it fascinating, and it will make the other party feel like you are closer to them. You will find that you can start leading by doing this so that after a short amount of time, they start copying you.

There are things about which you must be vigilant here. If someone else is slouching and gloomy, then copying might not benefit them; instead, you should take a similar approach so that they can begin to act more like you, then open it up and try to smile. Similarly, if they seem hostile or antagonistic towards you then strive not to imitate them, but also avoid offending them by taking the higher road with a more uplifting body language form. By being cool and not manipulating or feeding another's rage, a good understanding of body language would allow you to disperse such a situation.

It is also important to remember that it is only a small part of the battle to imitate their body. You need to have some substance to what you are saying, or else they might be puzzled as to why someone they are struggling to speak to copies their every move. Try to return to the person later when you have more resources if things are still not normal.

The next time you are out for lunch, shopping, or train, good exercise. Look at other people who chat or just sit next to each other and may be strangers. You will note that they relate to the positions of their arms and legs, the speed and intensity at which they are speaking, as well as how immediately after the other party will follow suit if one party moves in a certain direction.

People make a general mistake when they first encounter someone they are trying to connect with their words by finding common grounds, only after this initial connection is established through verbal communication can people then get in touch on a nonverbal level. The key is to build relationships first through body language on a nonverbal level and then move through verbal communication into building relationships.

Another great exercise to do the next time you speak to someone, whether they are someone you have known for a long time or just met. Note the body language of each other, and you will note whether or not you are in a relationship; usually, after 5-10 minutes of conversation, some sort of nonverbal relationship will be formed. If you do, you will start leading in the mirroring and matching, or as they call it, entrainment. What this means is that you can move your arm or leg in a certain position or movement and continue with the conversation as soon as you realize that the other party has unintentionally changed into the same gesture or posture; this is the strength of the relationship.

Breathing in harmony with the other party is the best mirror that can build relationships. In a business or social setting, this may be much harder to do, but it is the most effective and discreet move to imitate. With your significant other, this is only used for the bathroom, check it out and thank me later! Breathing in unison does not just mean the same number of breaths, but also where the other person breathes in the body, whether shallow breathing to the chest and deep breathing to the abdomen. Should they breathe through the mouth or the nose? In what way do they inhale and exhale?

Another important factor to consider is proximity; each has different levels of comfort depending on how near or distant others are in contact with each other. We all know the one person who loves to stand up in our face and spit on us literally as they speak, but others are more comfortable talking at a distance where we can barely touch them with our hands.

Physical touch is the second strongest way to build relationships, which can build more relationships than anything you have ever written. Nonetheless, this is more difficult to apply in a job environment; you might want to save this for later until you are more suited and confident to use it in social settings.

If you are on the phone a lot, then you are going to want to concentrate more on the auditory elements, including voice tone, speed, rhythm, volume, jargon, and keywords.

Dating / Relationship

Reporting on a date is vital, but it is also crucial that you do not live in your head and just copy your friend. Mirroring is best done when something does not fit well, and you note that you are out of sync physically but do not necessarily test their actions and mirror everything they do. You can try to be yourself as much as you can because it is nice to have plenty of gift-and-take in a relationship; you do not just want to imitate them. Strong communication, however, will ensure that things go smoothly.

If it is good to look for encouraging signs on a date and if things feel like they are going well, then go on the same path, but do not just repeat yourself or you risk alienating or upsetting the other person. One of the most dangerous considerations in evaluating a date is that many of the positive behaviors like playing with hair or shyness can also be indicators of discomfort or dissatisfaction. You should be able to pick out whether these things are good or bad, depending on whether they are geared towards or away from you and whether there are power and joy that reciprocates them. Like with many of these guidelines on body language, it is best to focus on yourself when you feel a lot of disconnects and then take further steps to reflect and observe. Once people connect, synchronization is very normal, so do not feel like it has to happen if it is not. When you try so hard to connect with someone, maybe it was not meant to be.

In Business And Job Interviews

Nonetheless, when actually in an interview, there is a deliberate power play to bear in mind. You need power and confidence to plan, but you also need to stroke your colleagues ' and potential employer's ego. When going to the meeting, when walking up to the building, keep a good posture and when sitting down, take up more space than normal (without being annoying) and maintain an upright posture, it is very good to take on power positions. Research has shown that performing power poses with testosterone and cortisol for a few minutes at a time produces biological effects at a hormonal level. Increasing the latter and arising from bad poses and increasing the former from power poses, leading to greater confidence.

When you are in the interviewer's house, make sure you are reading how they are doing. In reality, most interviewers feel very nervous and are happy that you are taking charge of the discussions and directing them in the right direction. That is not always the case, but do not always presume that they are in charge and do not want you to be in the role. Whether or not you are expected to mimic in this situation can be difficult to judge because you want to build a good level of partnership. After all, you do not want to look weak or disrespectful when they are confident and assertive, yet you do not want to announce that you are fair if they do not think that is the case yet, and just because they are comfortable does not mean you are supposed to be the same.

The most important thing to remember is to keep constant contact with the face and eyes without scaring the other person and keep a good stance on the ground with your feet attached. Hold your breathing steady and let your hands talk a lot as long as they do not shake like wind leaves. Whatever you do, remember to schedule the interview correctly and maintain a good degree of charm and language of the body throughout the interview.

CHAPTER - 10

INTERPRETATION OF GESTURES IN LOVE

You may be insanely attracted to a person but may not have the courage to ask them out owing to the prospect of facing humiliation and rejection. Imagine how easier things would be if you knew if they are as much into you as you are into them. Think of a situation where you've been set up on a blind date by enthusiastic friends, or you find a date online, and really want to know if they are attracted to you. You may go out on a first date and come back not knowing whether the person really liked you or not!

Wouldn't it be nice if there could be a telepathic way to gauge if a person feels truly attracted to you? How can you figure out if a person is genuinely attracted to you or is being plain nice to you because they don't want to hurt you (yes, we've all been guilty of this.)

Can verbal and non-verbal clues help you establish a potential lover's true feelings, emotions, thoughts, and intentions? Can body language be used for unlocking a person's subconscious mind to tune in to their innermost feelings and thoughts about you? Use these secret attraction clues (that I rarely share with anyone) to help you gain and increase social proof and experience more gratifying and fulfilling relationships.

The Attraction Signals

When an individual is attracted to you, they will transmit plenty of feel-good or positive non-verbal clues for you to tune in to at a subconscious level.

To begin with, when a person is deeply attracted to you, their bodies will almost always face you.

Everything from their face, the chest to shoulders and feet will most likely be pointed in your direction. The person will lean closer while speaking or interacting with you in a bid to get closer on a subconscious and emotional level. When they stand at a distance of under four feet away from you, they are keen on entering or personal space or inner circle of friends. They are trying to physically enter your inner zone or personal space to make a place for themselves in it.

If you want to know if a person is keenly into you or interested in you, don't give in to their interest straight away. Rather than facing them, maintain a shoulder to shoulder position. If the person is truly interested in you, he or she will make an effort to win your attraction. Let them know that they have to win your attraction for you to stand facing them or mirror their attraction signals.

Leaning in the direction of a person is almost always a sign of attraction. We subconsciously lean towards people we are attracted to. When a person leans towards you in a group, it is clear that they are interested in you (or what you are speaking). Of course, sometimes a person may be simply keen on listening to what you are saying, in which case, you will have to look at other clues. However, leaning towards a person within a group setting is a subconscious indication that they are drawn towards you.

Another sign of attraction includes seizing a person from up to down, and then down to up. This is a primitive way, yet still practiced, for checking out the sexual potential of a prospective mate.

Together with other clues, uncrossed arms and legs can be a sign of attraction. Similarly, a broad smile, dilated pupils, and open palms can also reveal attraction. Head tilting is another sign of interest and engagement. It signals a person's desire to communicate to you that they are always around for you. Looking at a person in the eye for long while speaking can also be a huge sign of attraction. If you are attracted to a person or want to win their affection, avoid looking over their heads or even all over the place. It reveals a lack of interest and sensitivity, which will not give them the right signal.

Touch

Touch is a clue that an individual is completely comfortable in your presence. They may also be keen or getting to know more about you. They may get flirtatious or hit on you by playfully touching you. Some of the most common initial attractions signals are placing their hand over your hand, brushing their shoulder or leg against your shoulder or leg while talking to you and pretending to touch you accidentally.

If you are confused about how to read a person's touches, observe how they touch another person versus how they touch you. If they are generally touchy-feely with everyone around, it is their baseline personality.

However, if they make special exceptions in the manner in which they touch you, it is more often than not, a sign of attraction. If the individual touches more than normal or in a different way, he or she may be attracted to you.

If you are attracted to a person, use body language to your advantage by conveying your feelings through non-verbal signals. Don't distance yourself from the person even if you don't want to send out very obvious signs of attraction.

On a subconscious level, they may not realize they are attracted to you. Similarly, don't go all out and make the person step back in discomfort. Maintain a balance. Start with a light or playful tap on the shoulder or elbows. It is harmless yet reveals that a person likes you. Then gradually, move to touch their arm, wrist or back while talking. Make the touch more gradual and subtle so they don't wince or retreat with discomfort.

Mirroring

Mirroring happens at a deeply subconscious level and is one of the most reliable signals of a person's attraction. Watch out for people mirroring your actions.

There is either a deep-seated need to be accepted or they are truly attracted to you. Sometimes after you've just met or been introduced to a person at a party, you'll notice that he or she starts mirroring everything from your words to your nods to your hand gestures to expressions.

People who don't know much about reading or analyzing people will often miss these clues.

However, on a subconscious level, this is a sign that the person is seeking your acceptance or approval. When you are leaning against the bar, you'll notice a person come up to you and lean in the same position as you before striking up a conversation. They are doing nothing but attempting to mirror your actions in a bid to make you feel that they are one among your kind. People will hold their glass exactly in the manner in which you are holding yours or they may take a sip on their drink right after you do to show you that they are like you. The feeling of affiliating with people on a psychological level drives people to mirror their actions.

CHAPTER - 11

EMOTIONAL

INTELLIGENCE

Emotional intelligence also referred to as emotional leadership or emotional quotient, is the ability of certain people to realize their emotions, as well as those of others, differentiate them, label, and readily manage or adjust depending on the situation or environment. These people typically remain calm despite the changes in the surrounding or negative impacts associated with a given case. Besides, they may apply the capability to help those affected by awkward feelings, therefore, making them feel at peace. Emotional intelligence is psychological, where one understands and handles any kind of emotion with ease while remaining calm.

Over the years, the definition of emotional intelligence was broken down into four sections: perceiving, utilizing, learning, and managing.

The four abilities were all attributed to emotional intelligence with relative meanings behind them. Different models were created using these abilities, therefore, facilitating how thoughts and understanding of emotions interact. Studies show that people with more emotional intelligence tend to succeed more in various areas, including academics, careers, and talents.

Since the introduction of emotional intelligence, different studies have been conducted with the objective of determining the actual factors driving an individual to manage emotions. Most of us react to varying feelings to some extent, depending on the severity or fun in it. However, higher emotional intelligence people have the ability to manage these emotions and have a minimal impact on their lives, even on extensive influences of a situation. With different groups of people, emotional intelligence has been seen to have different implications on the thoughts of these individuals. For instance, children and teens with high emotional intelligence tend to have good social interaction while those having lower abilities have the opposite. Adults with high emotional intelligence accompany an excellent self-perception socially while those with low emotional intelligence tend to become aggressive.

Features of Emotional Intelligence

- **Show of Authenticity**

High emotional intelligence people, especially those who are more social, tend to stick to their principles and values. When sharing about themselves to others, they usually stand by their boundaries rather than sharing everything about themselves to others. As such, authenticity does not imply that you have to share all about yourself. However, you share about yourself to people who matter and those who understand you and appreciate your thoughts and feelings.

- **Demonstration of Empathy**

These individuals tend to demonstrate empathy to people as they readily understand other people's feelings and thoughts. They, therefore, readily connect to others and agree on what is essential. Emotional intelligence enables them to develop more profound and more productive relationships with others. Instead of becoming judgmental and avoiding those who feel different, they comfort and make them feel important to society. Despite being empathetic, these people are cautious when it comes to decision making, therefore avoiding agreeing to every person's motive.

- **Apologetic and Forgiving**

Another feature of emotional intelligence people is that they quickly understand their mistakes. They usually have the courage and strength to apologize even without errors, therefore, indicating value to a relationship. The same applies to forgive and forget, even in the most resentful situations. As such, having emotional intelligence provides a mind that readily forgives and free from your emotions from those who hurt you.

- **Being Helpful**

As emotional intelligence entails understanding and managing your emotions and that of others, then helping them becomes part of what the ability accompanies. As one of the most significant rewards to others, helping becomes a habit to these people, and they never tire or discriminate against others. However, they help each person in need without asking too many questions. As such, it helps those who follow similar footsteps as well as building trust among people to help others.

- **Always Thinking About Feelings**

Emotional intelligence primarily dwells on one's feelings which often change suddenly or slowly depending on the situation or environment. When an individual has a higher emotional intelligence capability, then he or she frequently thinks about different feelings and how it may impact others. They usually ask about common questions regarding their self-awareness, reflecting on everyday activities, and people who may be influenced by their emotions. As such, systematic thinking and learning about emotions provide insights used to their advantage in managing their feelings and that of others.

- **Benefit from Criticism**

Nobody experiences fun when it comes to negative feedback, especially from people you trust and those close to you. However, these types of reputation are quite effective in life as they teach you a few lessons about a particular aspect. Besides, it enables you to learn more about how others think mainly about you and things to change and become better in what you do. Receiving these negative feedbacks may become a challenge to others, but those with the ability to check their emotions benefit a lot. With the use of emotional intelligence, these people can learn to manage their emotions and move around calmly without focusing on the thoughts of others.

Managing Emotions

- ### People with Low Emotional Intelligence

When low emotional intelligence people are faced with any negative emotion, they tend to become violent or rather more reactive when compared to those with high emotional intelligence. For instance, when an individual with low emotional intelligence faces negative criticism, they may initially go into denial and withdraw from a given group to avoid shame. They become lonely and prevent any form of help offered towards them. In some cases, others may opt to use substances to keep their minds active and evade others and what they are feeling. Others may harm themselves by cutting, starving, purging, or engaging in dangerous behaviors. The primary drive to these activities is influenced by a lack of control of emotions which are usually hurting, such as criticism.

- ### People with High Emotional Intelligence

High emotional intelligence people have all it takes to absorb and express reasonably about how they feel about a particular sensation. For instance, when these group people are offended, they would initially pause before acting and think what their next word or rather the best harmless action to take. They would also acknowledge what the next person is feeling or have in mind before deciding on providing their contribution or conclusion of what will become. Thinking first is usually their first step to prevent escalating the problem or causing more harm to themselves and others. Another critical aspect of high emotional intelligence people is helping themselves and people affected by a given emotion. In this case, high emotional intelligence people act entirely different when compared to low emotional intelligence individuals.

Emotional Quotient (EQ) Vs. Intelligence Quotient (IQ)

Emotional Quotient, EQ, is the ability of an individual to readily learn, understand, handle, and control his or her emotions even in the most resentful situations. On the other hand, Intelligence Quotient, IQ, is the measure of one's intelligence usually expressed in a number. EQ enables an individual to focus on emotions which, in turn, acts as a management system to different emotions which may become harmful to others. More so, it involves other people's emotions, and an individual can readily manage these emotions without the need to sympathize. IQ measures the degree of intelligence calculated from standardized tests created to analyze human intelligence.

Components of Emotional Intelligence

Emotional intelligence is linked to different internal components of a person usually within the brain, which determines how one understands and controls emotions. In most cases, people who lack control of their emotions have been associated with mental problems. While others stating that lack of emotional control is attributed to the extent of the immediate feeling at hand. However, emotional intelligence has been proven to exist among different individuals and comprises the following components.

- **Self-Awareness**

This is the ability to recognize and learn about your emotions as well as understanding the effects accompanied by your feelings. Becoming self-aware is determined by being able to monitor emotions, realizing emotional reactions, and identifying each emotion independently. Besides, you readily understand and figure out the interaction between your emotions and how you behave when that feeling occurs. That is, when you are an emotionally intelligent individual, you become aware of several aspects about yourself and others while keeping in mind about what is wrong and right. You can readily make a choice to do wrong or wicked despite how sad, angry, or hopeless you become.

Self-awareness also builds the ability to determinethestrengthsandlimitationsforquick development of measures to avoid negative impacts to an individual and to others. As a person, you can get access to new information and personal skills; therefore, you learn from others. People with a sense of self-awareness are usually humorous, confident, and aware of the perception of others. More so, they understand what it means to be emotional despite being an everyday behavior. As among the primary components of emotional intelligence, self-awareness provides a complete guide to an individual to quickly learn what to do when facing a given emotion, which may harm both them and another person when mishandled.

- **Self-Regulation**

Another significant component of emotional intelligence is self-regulation, which entails the regulation and management of emotions. After becoming self-aware of your feelings and the accompanying impacts to others and yourself, you are required to have a governing force that enhances how you react during these situations. However, it does not imply that an individual has to lock away his or her real emotions and hide how they feel about others, but they should express them in an organized manner. That is, regulating how you express your feelings in an appropriate time and place.

People skilled in self-regulation are mostly flexible and quickly adapt to change as well as excellent in settling disagreements among people and diffusion of tension. More so, they are high in conscientiousness, thoughtful, and take responsibility for their doings. As a component of emotional intelligence, self-regulation plays a significant role in enabling an individual to quickly manage and handle all types of feelings, either positive or negative, without influencing others negatively.

- **Social Skills**

Emotional intelligence also comprises of social skills which are the ability to interact with others correctly. Learning about your feelings and that of others, and being able to control is not enough to develop your emotional intelligence. Then, there is a need to implement these abilities into actions when interacting with others daily. When you indulge in daily communication with others and put into action this information, then you are at the forefront in managing your feelings and that of others. For example, managers in businesses have utilized the knowledge of social skills to interact with workers and clients, thus benefiting significantly in their careers.

- **Empathy**

Empathy is the capability of comprehending other individual's feelings. It is also vital to emotional intelligence but provides more insight to an individual rather than recognizing the emotions of others. Empathy involves realizing emotions as well as reactions to these emotions, which primarily encompasses the help needed. For example, if someone is hopeless, sad, or emotional dependent, you are likely to sense these emotions and respond accordingly as if they are yours. You tend to provide extra care and concern, allowing other people to recognize power dynamics that influence relationships. Therefore, emotional intelligence enables you to become empathetic to others and give the needed support.

CHAPTER - 12

EMOTIONAL

MANIPULATION

What is Emotional Manipulation?

Now that we have covered the basic foundations of dark psychology, including the concept of seriously dangerous psychopathy and the irreversible movement toward the Dark Singularity, you may feel a sense of relief that these societal problems have been identified, and that a system for addressing them has been established. In addition, you may also breathe a sigh of relief knowing that the most serious offenders are somewhat rare, and that your chances of encountering them on a daily basis are fairly low.

If you agree that knowledge of the traits of dark psychology is a good first step toward protecting yourself from these dangers—that's great! Knowledge is power, more so in the information age than ever.

However, the truth of dark psychology is that lower levels of these deviant personality traits are extremely common. Worse yet, they are often legitimized by the very institutions and people we depend upon to address such violations. Especially in the contemporary environment, in which technology has fostered and encouraged the development of alienation and anti-social lifestyles to the unprecedented degree that they now provide a potentially viable and sustainable means of financial and social support, understanding how dark psychology manifests itself can make the difference between success and failure.

Types of Emotional Manipulation

Discussing manipulative behavior accurately requires that we examine this problem from two perspectives: from the perspective of clinical psychology and from the perspective of every-day relationships. We will begin by discussing different types of emotional manipulation using clinical terminology.

Many clinical psychologists have studied and classified manipulative behavior according to well-established theories of behavior modification and cognitive learning. We will look first at some of the techniques identified by a few of these psychologists before looking at real-world examples and signs that someone is trying to manipulate you.

Characteristics of a Manipulative Relationship

First, one theory states that emotional manipulation is essentially a one-sided activity in which all of the effort to create, execute, and sustain a manipulative relationship is made by the manipulator. Such relationships generally have three defining characteristics:

1. **Concealment:** The true motivations of the manipulator—aggression and control—are concealed by behavior that appears friendly and helpful.

It is more difficult to conceal problems with aggression and control in our personal, intimate relationships, our friendships, and our relationships among family members. As a result, these types of relationships are more likely to develop in the workplace or in your community among business owners and their staff or other professionals.

For example, you may encounter a co-worker who, on the surface, is always friendly toward you at work. This person may always be willing to find a place for you at the table during lunch break or may always appear at your cubicle with a smile and offer lots of encouragement and advice. This type of conduct in itself may be a good sign. However, if this relationship ultimately leads to a friendship outside of the office, an emotional manipulator may misinterpret your intent.

In the less-regulated world outside of the workplace, emotional predators may exploit the trust they have established by making unreasonable demands on your time, asking for favors, and putting pressure on you to agree by suggesting there could be repercussions at work. A truly gifted manipulator will know how to make this threatening behavior look and feel friendly and perfectly reasonable until you have been too badly compromised to take any action to reverse course.

1. **Profiling:** The manipulator will have studied the vulnerabilities of the victim, so that he or she will be able to exploit them more effectively.

This type of predatory conduct has become much worse in the current environment of surveillance and social networking sites.

Often in the work environment, this type of personality can manifest itself without your awareness. Especially if you work for a large company, anyone who has access to personnel records or other sources of information may feel they have the luxury to profile you so that when they do finally approach, they will appear quite calm and confident.

If someone with whom you have had little or no direct contact seems to know a lot about you, you should be cautious. Often, being overly enthusiastic, paying you a lot of compliments, and telling you that you have earned a great reputation is a technique used to hide the true intentions of the manipulator.

- **Amorality:** The manipulator will possess high degrees of amorality and a lack of remorse, both of which enable behavior that is ruthless, cunning, and treacherous.

Often, we expect that a simple, polite request to cease harmful, rude, or disruptive behavior should be sufficient to end predatory or violative misconduct. Although we may be right, Dark Triad personalities who lack empathy find it easy to engage in amoral behavior. Even worse, far from feeling any remorse as a result of committing abuses, they often feel a great sense of joy, victory, and accomplishment. As the saying goes, such reactions add insult to injury.

Further, in the competitive business environment, this type of dishonest and illegal behavior may be rewarded. Meanwhile, the efforts of diligent, honest employees may go unrewarded, and their complaints of abuse may result in punishments levied against them rather than the perpetrators.

Categories of Emotionally Manipulative Behavior

Understanding the basic dynamics of manipulative and abusive relationships is important. Each of these general types of relationships may be characterized by specific types of behavior. Psychologists have identified many specific techniques of behavior modification commonly employed by emotional manipulators. Some of these techniques include:

- **Positive reinforcement:** This technique was identified by the behavioral psychologist B.F. Skinner, whose theory of operant conditioning resulted from his experiments with small animals placed in cages. In his experiment to prove the theory of positive reinforcement, he used cages equipped with two levers—one lever did nothing, while the other produced a food pellet whenever the small animal pushed it. Soon, the animals learned through positive reinforcement which lever to push to get their reward.

Emotional manipulators employ positive reinforcement in their strategies by using techniques such as praise, false and superficial demonstrations of emotions such as charm and sympathy, excessive rewards including gifts, money, approval, and attention, and other outward demonstrations of emotion meant to make the victim feel good.

- **Negative reinforcement:** The other part of Skinner's experiment proved the effectiveness of negative reinforcement. For this part of his experiment, small animals were again placed in cages, which were again equipped with two levers. This time, the cages were charged with a mild voltage of electricity that caused slight discomfort to the animals that were placed in them. Once inside the cages, the animals would press one of the two levers. One of the levers did not produce any results, while the other stopped the electrical current, relieving the discomfort. Soon, the animals learned to press the lever that lessened their pain.

Emotional manipulators employ negative reinforcement in their strategies by using techniques such as removing someone from a difficult situation or relieving them of the responsibility to complete a previously agreed job or task in exchange for some type of favor.

Intermittent reinforcement: Intermittent reinforcement can be either positive or negative and is used to create doubt, fear, or uncertainty. An emotional manipulator may "train" his or her victim by imposing inconsistent reward and punishment mechanisms to lessen the victim's sense of confidence, control, and autonomy.

For example, in a romantic relationship, the predator may condition the victim to wear certain clothing, listen to certain music, eat certain types of food, and work at a certain type of job. As the victim in this relationship gains confidence, the predator may begin to discourage their victim, who will be caught off guard. As the victim scrambles to respond, the manipulator may again change tactics.

- **Punishment:** Punishment is a very basic form of emotional manipulation that may involve an entire range of psychologically and emotionally negative and damaging behavior, such as threats, yelling, nagging, complaining, intimidation, insults, guilt, and other forms of emotional blackmail. Skilled predators may find a way to incorporate this abusive and controlling behavior into the relationship over time, so that the victim will develop a tolerance for abuse.

- **Traumatic one-trial learning:** This technique is related to the use of punishments, but rather than a feature of a long-term relationship, these techniques involve discrete episodes in which the manipulator uses verbal abuse, demonstrations of anger, and other forms of dominance and intimidation to discourage the victim from certain types of behavior.

CHAPTER - 13

NON-VERBAL COMMUNICATION

While the best approach to achievement in your associations is in the ability to speak properly, it is not about the words but rather it is the nonverbal sign or nonverbal communication that is the most extraordinary. Nonverbal communication is the usage of physical direct, verbalizations, and peculiarities to grant nonverbally, routinely done instinctually instead of purposefully.

Despite whether you are aware of it or not, when you work together with others, you are continually offering and tolerating quiet hint. Most of your nonverbal practices, the sign you make, your position, your way of talking, how much eye to eye association you make, send strong messages. They can comfort people, manufacture conviction and bring people closer to you, or they can affront, perplex, and undercut what you are endeavoring to pass on.

When you stop talking, the messages do not stop. Despite when you are peaceful, in spite of all that you are passing on nonverbally.

In specific events, what leaves your mouth and what you pass on through your nonverbal communication may be two exceptionally astonishing things. If you express a specific something, yet your nonverbal communication is different, your group of spectators will presumably assume that you are being exploitative. In case you state yes but you are shaking your head to indicate 'no', for example. Exactly when looked with mixed signals, the group of spectators needs to pick whether to acknowledge your nonverbal or verbal message. Since nonverbal communication is a trademark, negligent language that conveys your genuine feelings and objectives, they will likely pick the message that is nonverbal.

Regardless, by bettering how you grasp and utilize nonverbal communication, it is possible to articulate what you actually mean, partner better with those around you, and production more grounded, all the additionally compensating associations.

For what reason does nonverbal communication have any kind of effect? Your nonverbal communication prompts, the way wherein you tune in and move, tell the individual you are talking with if you really think about it, on the off chance that you are being straightforward, and how well you are tuning in. Right when your nonverbal sign aligns with the words being expressed, they guarantee conviction, lucidity, and affection. If they do not, they can make weight, uncertainty, and perplexity.

If you have to improve as a communicator, then it is basic to end up being logically fragile not only to the nonverbal communication and nonverbal sign of others, yet notwithstanding your own.

Nonverbal Communication Will Expect the Following Roles:

Substitution: It can stand-in for a verbal message. For instance, the outward appearance you portray much of the time passes on an obviously more striking message than words ever can.

Irregularity: It can disavow the message you are endeavoring to pass on, thusly exhibiting to your group of spectators that you may not be telling the truth.

Repetition: It recurs and regularly supports the verbal message.

Supplementing: It may underscore a verbal message. For example, repeatedly knocking on the table will emphasize the criticalness of the message you intend to communicate.

Enhancing: It may increase to or supplement the verbal message you communicate. As a chief, if you pat a delegate on the back despite giving acknowledgment, it can extend the impact of your message.

Types of Nonverbal Communication

There a wide scope of sorts of nonverbal communication or nonverbal communication include:

- **Gestures – These have been woven into our lives. You might speak animatedly; argue with your hands, point, wave, or beckon. Gestures do change according to cultures.**

- **Facial expressions – You will learn that the face is expressive and able to show several emotions without speaking one word. Unlike what you say and other types of body language, facial expressions are usually universal.**

- **Eye contact – Because sight tends to be our strongest sense for most people, it is an important part of Non-verbal communication. The way someone looks at you could tell you whether they are attracted to you, affectionate, hostile, or interested. It might also help the conversation flow.**

- **Body movement and posture – Take a moment to think about how you view people based on how they hold their heads, stand, walk around, and sit. The way a person carries gives you a lot of information.**

Non-verbal communication could go wrong in several different ways. It is very easy to confuse different signals, and the rest of this chapter will make sure that won't happen.

How Non-verbal Communication Can Turn Out Severely

What you pass on through your nonverbal communication and nonverbal sign will influence what others think about you. It is necessary to take into consideration the manner in which you are communicating as this guarantees that people see you in a specific light. Nonverbal communication is likely to tell somebody else a lot about you than you can ever tell them in speech.

Could Nonverbal Communication Be Phony?

There are various books and locales that offer direction on the most ideal approach to use nonverbal communication facilitating your potential advantage. For example, they may teach you on the most ideal approach to position yourself in a specific way, the movement of your fingers or any other body movement that will influence how somebody else looks at you. Regardless, truth be told, such snares are not most likely getting down to business, aside from on the off chance that you really feel certain and in charge.

You must carefully consider your communication because it will give other people an instant chance to develop an opinion about yourself. If you make a body movement without actually meaning to communicate a specific message, it might confuse them and characterize it as phone communication. For example, if you twist your face, it should indicate anger and this is the first impression that somebody is likely to have of you. It is necessary to take into consideration what you really want to communicate in order to be effective and allow other people to think of you in a specific way.

On the off chance that you need to convey adequately, stay away from misconceptions, and appreciate strong, confiding seeing someone both socially and expertly, it is critical to see how to utilize and decipher nonverbal communication and improve your nonverbal relational abilities.

The Most Effective Method to Improve Nonverbal Communication

Nonverbal communication is a quickly streaming forward and backward procedure that requires your concentration in order to communicate a specific message with others. It is necessary to think before you act so that your nonverbal communication is effective and allows people to think of you in a specific way. Do not be too quick to act because you will cause confusion; take into consideration your own body movements as you communicate. Most people ignore the simple fact that their nonverbal communication will communicate more than want they are saying, so thinking before you act is extremely important.

Assessing Non-verbal Signs

Power – Does the individual appear to be level, cool, and impartial, or over-the-top and sensational?

Outward appearance – How does their visage look? Does it look like they are wearing a mask or showing a sense of sincerity?

Eye to eye connection – Is the individual looking? Provided that this is true, is it excessively exceptional or without flaw?

Manner of speaking – Are they clear and sensible when they communicate or do you feel as though they are hiding something from you?

Resonance – Do you hear sounds that demonstrate enthusiasm, mindful or worry from the individual?

Stance and signal – Do they look tense as indicated by raised shoulders, do they seem uncomfortable in any way when they speak?

Contact – Are they making any physical constant with you, and more importantly, are you comfortable with it?

Timing– Is there a simple progression of data forward and backward? Do nonverbal reactions come too rapidly or too gradually?

CHAPTER - 14

CAN I LEARN HOW TO FAKE MY BODY LANGUAGE?

Some people feel that faking this kind of thing is impossible. They know that it is hard to hide a lot of the body signs that you are trying to show to others. This doesn't mean that the process is impossible to work with, but it does take a lot of time and effort to do.

Many people are not aware of the different body languages and nonverbal language cues that they send out to the world. But this doesn't mean that you are not able to fake some of it, and get others to think that you feel and act in a certain way. Keep in mind here that doing this is going to be difficult sometimes. It is not always as easy as it seems, and you have to be constantly aware of what you are doing. If you forget to do this and aren't paying attention to the different parts of your body language and how they are working together, you will find that some part of you will betray you, and you lose the trust in the person you are trying to work with.

Some of the things that you should focus on include:

The Eye Contact

The first thing that we are going to focus on when we need to fake our body language is going to be eye contact. You need to make sure that your eye contact is on point. This is one of the easiest things to fake, and if you are messing up with this still in your personal and professional life, then it means that you are going to have to work on that before you get a chance to work with some of the others.

Think about the last time you talked with someone who was not able to maintain eye contact. Whether it was them focusing down all of the time, them looking at their phone or their watch, or even glancing towards the door all of the time, it felt like they wanted to look anywhere but at you. Eventually, it made you feel like you were not important, and you wanted to stop the conversation and move on, no matter how important the information was.

Don't be like this person. You don't want to make the other person feel like they are not important. You want them to know that you are interested in them, that what they have to say is worth your attention. And the best way to do this is to make sure that your eye contact is good.

There is a nice balance here. You do not want your gaze to be so intense that you make the other person feel uncomfortable. We all know this kind of gaze. It includes no blinking and may feel like you are trying to do a stare down with the other person. Focus on a gaze that shows that you are interested, but include some blinking and some emotion in them as well.

Your Arm Movements

Pay attention to the arm movements that you are doing. If you want to be able to show another person that you are excited and happy about something, it probably is not a good idea to stand with the arms crossed. Happiness and excitement are going to include a lot of arm movements going all of the time. The bigger the movements (within reason, don't try to hit the other person with the flailing arms), the more animated you are going to appear to others as well.

However, if you want to appear like you are calm and collected, or like you are more withdrawn (there may be times when you want someone to leave you alone for example), then crossing your arms, or at least keeping the arms and hands close to the body, may be the right option for your needs.

If you want to show that you are animated and excited, then the arm movements need to be away from the body and nice and big. If you're going to show that you are more withdrawn, then the arms and hands need to be close to the body.

The Smile

It is important to spend some time focusing on the smile that you give off. Many of us have been trained on how to give a fake smile in any situation, but there is a big difference between the fake smile and a genuine smile. You may be able to fake it with some people, but often, you need to try and get a real and genuine smile on your face to impress those around you.

Remember that with a genuine smile, you need to use more than the sides of the mouth. This one includes the whole face and even some crinkles around the eyes. This can be done even when faking it, but you need to do some practice. An excellent way to do this is to spend some time in a mirror, working on the smile, and trying to get the whole face into it.

Doing a smile in front of the mirror is going to make a big difference. You can look at how the smile will appear to others, and get a general feel of how it is going to feel to do this. Then, when you are in front of someone else using this smile, without the mirror present, you will know how to make this smile appear for you.

Your Stance

The last thing that we are going to look at is your stance. You need to make sure that you are picking out the right kind of stance to impress another person and let them know that you are interested. Of course, the posture is going to be an important part of all of this. You want to stand upright, rather than to slouch, and you want to make sure that you show off the confidence that is inside of you.

There is more to this one than just the posture that you use, though. If you can add a few more things into this, you will find out that it is going to help you to get some results with how comfortable others are around you. The first thing to look at is your feet. If you want the other person to think that you are interested in them and that your whole attention is on them, then make sure the feet are pointed in the right direction. They need to be pointed at the person you are talking to, rather than to the side or even worse, towards the door.

The way that you lean is important as well. If your posture has you leaning towards the door, or at all away from the other person, then this is going to give them the thought that you are not interested in them at all. But, if you are leaning slightly towards them, with your body leaning in, it shows that you are interested in what they are saying to them.

It is hard to fake the body language that you are doing with another person. While we often wish to show off a certain kind of appearance to others, it is going to be tough to do this. You have to be careful about how you do this.

CHAPTER - 15

NEURO-LINGUISTIC PROGRAMMING (NLP)

Neuro-Linguistic Programming has to do with the study of thoughts (neuro) and language (linguistic) in a systemic way and the scripts that run the life of an individual (programming).

It deals with the understanding and the development of the mind and the entire understanding of the language of the mind in relation to the way it is designed to function and the ways in which it is molded by the personal experiences of an individual. It is simply a study of a person's subjective reality.

A proper understanding of the language of the mind influences every aspect of a person's life from his relationship with others to his communication skills with friends and clients to the general outcome of a person's life. It is a holistic study that puts the spirit, body, past and present of an individual into consideration.

As homo sapiens who are gifted with the ability to think, it is presumed that our most important function is the thought or the thinking function. NLP, however, brings one to the understanding of the fact that no thought process exists in a vacuum, as they are a product of a person's perspective. It has a presupposition of perception as reality and it holds that the things, we think are colored by the way we think.

For different individuals there are different ways of thinking and interpreting reality. What NLP does is assist in the understanding of these various representational systems to help each person narrow down his own system. It helps in the understanding of the three different types of thinking patterns which are:

- Visual: deals with both pictures and visual metaphors.

- Auditory: sound (hearing).

- Kinesthetic: deals with the five senses, as well as gut feelings.

In NLP, a person is thought to take absolute control of his mind and ultimately his life. Unlike what is obtainable in psychoanalysis, which places its focus on "why," NLP presents a more practical approach with its focus on the "how."

How NLP Works

If you are just coming across this topic for the first time, NLP may appear or seem like magic or hypnosis. When a person is undergoing therapy, this topic digs deep into the unconscious mind of the patient and filters through different layers of beliefs and the person's approach or perception of life to deduce the early childhood experiences that are responsible for a behavioral pattern.

In NLP, it is believed that everyone has the resources that are needed for positive changes in their own lives. The technique adopted here is meant to help in facilitating these changes.

Usually, when NLP is taught, it is done in a pyramidal structure. However, the most advanced techniques are left for those multi-thousand-dollar seminars. An attempt to explain this complicated subject is to state that the NLPer (as those who use NLP will often call themselves) is always paying keen attention to the person they are working on/with.

Usually, there is a large majority of NLPers that are therapists and they are very likely to be well-meaning people. They achieve their aims by paying attention to those subtle cues like the movement of the eyes, flushing of the skin, dilation of the pupil and subtle nervous tics. It is easy for an NLP user to quickly determine the following:

- The side of the brain that the person uses predominantly.

- The sense (smell, sight, etc.) that is more dominant in a person's brain.

- The way the person's brain stores and makes use of information (the NLPer can deduce all this from the person's eye movement).

- When they are telling a lie or concocting information.

When the NLP user has successfully gathered all this information, they begin to mimic the client in a slow and subtle manner by not only taking on their body language, but also by imitating their speech and mannerisms, so that they begin to talk with the language patterns that are aimed at targeting the primary senses of the client. They will typically fake the social cues that will easily make someone let their guard down so that they become very open and suggestible.

For example, when a person's sense of sight is their most dominant sense, the NLPer will use a language that is very laden with visual metaphors to speak with them. They will say things like: "do you see what I am talking about?" or "why not look at it this way?" For a person that has a more dominant sense of hearing, he will be approached with an auditory language like: "listen to me" or "I can hear where you're coming from."

To create a rapport, the NLPer mirrors the body language and the linguistic patterns of the other person. This rapport is a mental and physiological state which a human being gets into when they lose guard of their social senses. It is done when they begin to feel like the other person who they are conversing with is just like them.

Once the NLPer have achieved this rapport, they will take charge of the interaction by leading it in a mild and subtle manner. Thanks to the fact that they have already mirrored the other person, they will now begin to make some subtle changes in order to gain a certain influence on the behavior of the person. This is also combined with some similar subtle language patterns which lead to questions and a whole phase of some other techniques.

At this point, the NLPer will be able to tweak and twist the person to whichever direction they so desire. This only happens if the other person can't deduce that there is something going on because they assume everything that is occurring is happening organically or that they have given consent to everything.

What this means is that it is quite hard to make

use of NLP to get other people to act out of character, but it can be used to get a person to give responses within their normal range of character. This may come in the form of getting them to donate to a charitable cause, or finally making the decision they had been putting off or getting them to go home with you for the night if they had considered it at some point.

At this point, what the NLP user seeks to do may be to either elicit or anchor. When they are eliciting, they make use of both leading and language to get the person to an emotional state of say, sadness. Once they can elicit this state, they can then lead it on with a physical cue by touching the other person's shoulder for example.

According to theory, whenever the NLP user touches the person's shoulder in the same manner, the same emotional state will resurface if they do it again. However, this is only made possible by the successful conditioning of the other person.

When undergoing NLP therapy, it is very possible for the therapist to adopt a content-free approach, which means the therapist can work effectively without taking a critical look at the problem or without even knowing about the problem at all. This means that there is room for privacy for the client as the therapist does not really need to be told about whichever event took place or whatever issue happened in the past.

Also, prior to the commencement of the therapy, there is an agreement which ensures that the therapist cannot disclose any information, hence the interaction between the therapist and the client remains confidential.

In NLP, there is the belief in the need for the perfection of the nature of human creation, so every client is encouraged to recognize the sensitivity of the senses and make use of them in responding to specific problems. As a matter of fact, NLP also holds the belief that it is possible for the mind to find cures to diseases and sicknesses.

The techniques employed by NLP have to do with a noninvasive, medicine-free therapy that enables the client to find out new ways of handling emotional issues such as low self-esteem, lack of confidence, anxiety and destructive relationship patterns. It is also a successful tool in effective bereavement counselling.

With its roots in the field of behavioral science, which was developed by Skinner, Pavlov and Thorndike, NLP makes use of the combination physiology and the unconscious mind to bring about change in the thought process and ultimately the behavior of a person.

The Importance of NLP

Neuro-Linguistic Programming is not only necessary for the understanding of a person's being, but it also helps in the understanding of the way an individual is. It helps a person to get deep into the root cause of the problem, as well as the foundation of their being.

Here are some other reasons why NLP is important:

- It helps people take responsibility for the things that they feel they may not be able to control. With the help of NLP, it is possible for a person to change the way they react to events of the past and have a certain level of control over their future.

- It is very important for people to be aware of the body language of the members of their inner circle, as well as those who they seek to do business with. With NLP, it is possible to make use of language with both control and purpose, and with this it is possible to have control over your life.

Remember, you cannot expect to make the same mistakes using the same mindset and hope to get different results. During an NLP session, the focus is placed entirely on the client as they are made the subject. This helps a lot because at the point where a person can deal with his or herself as a person, they gain more clarity into his or her dealings with other people.

- It helps to improve finance, sales performance, marriage, health issues, parenting, customer service and every other aspect and phase of life. This is because it helps in the holistic improvement of an individual and when a person is whole, his interactions and relationship with himself and other people become whole as well.

- It assists in targeting your beliefs, thoughts and values and helps with the targeting of a person's brain functions, as well as developing certain behaviors. It also shapes the way these behaviors metamorphoses into habits and how the habits change to actions which in turn comes as results.

NLP is applicable in different vocations and professions. This is a tool that is very important in the mastery of sales, personal development experts and self-help, teaching, communication, parenting and other facets of life.

CHAPTER - 16

ETHICAL

MANIPULATION

The term 'manipulation' is defined as the art of influencing a subject to act in a certain way that is not common to them in order to achieve an objective. Whenever the term 'manipulation' is mentioned, many people almost immediately think of coercion or something similarly evil. This is wrong and unwholesome, as manipulation is not necessarily a negative thing. Manipulative techniques are currently used by several leaders in business and the government to achieve positive results for a common good. Nonetheless, it takes knowledge and a degree of training to be able to use the techniques of ethical manipulation productively.

In light of the above definitions, the term 'Ethical Manipulation' therefore refers to the exertion of influence to achieve a positive end goal. Emotional intelligence and Ethical Manipulation go hand-in-hand, as they both rely on a certain understanding to influence people in a particular direction.

Techniques of ethical manipulation are driven by the attainment of clearly-defined objectives. Herein lies the difference between ethical and unethical manipulation: the former is used as a means of helping others to achieve a common goal, while the latter is used for selfish gain, and this is inappropriate.

How to engage ethical manipulation

To influence people:

The power of emotional intelligence helps you influence people to a certain extent, but so does ethical manipulation. The methods are solely directed at influencing people to do things that they would not normally do on their own in order to achieve something worthwhile. Ethical manipulative techniques involve the use of appropriate pressure and direction to bring about desirable behaviors and outcomes in individuals.

To persuade people:

Ethical manipulation techniques are typically used to persuade people to see things from your own perspective, especially in situations of great controversy. When everyone at the table has a totally different opinion about a matter, it is unwise to try to forcefully impose your will on them, even if you have the power. So, to sell your perspective to them and ensure they buy it, ethical manipulation techniques offer you a chance to state your claims clearly in a way that their emotional strings pull their minds and hearts in your direction.

To inspire people:

People need to be inspired to achieve results. For instance, when people around you are lacking in confidence due to the size of a massive task before them, one way to help their crisis is to give them smaller and easier tasks to do. As they walk through each of them, chances are that their confidence levels may rise again, and they'd then become more optimistic of their chances at the big task.

To unify people:

It is not uncommon to experience strife in the workplace. However, a knowledge of ethical manipulation can help you influence people towards a peaceful resolution and coexistence. Preempt conflicts before they break out and take proactive measures to unify groups or teams.

Understanding What Triggers Behaviors

The goal of mastering emotional intelligence and ethical manipulation techniques is to be more influential. However, one of the greatest keys to becoming more influential is to not just interpret people's behavior, but to understand what triggers behaviors, both in ourselves and in other people.

Understanding the source and nature of the behaviors is much deeper than simply interpreting behaviors in context.

Human behavior is birthed in the mind. Humans have both a conscious part and a subconscious one. Now, there aren't actually two minds; no, they are only two aspects of our minds. Interestingly, the majority of what we do and the way we behave comes from the subconscious part of our mind. In fact, the realm of the subconscious is far wider and more real than the conscious, and many things we do are controlled from there.

There are many things we do that we are conscious about. However, there are several things that we do without knowing, and it is only after a while that our conscious self-catches up with reality to discern the activity and impact of the subconscious. This is why many people give off body language signals without even knowing. It's their subconscious at work there.

Human behavior is inspired by four Cardinal elements: emotions, feelings, thoughts and beliefs, all intangible and within the realm of the mind. No action occurs without a cause and a context. And even though we may not always be conscious of the cause, the fact that there's a cause behind every action still remains valid.

Feelings of sadness or unhappiness make people react in a specific way. They respond based on how they feel, or what they believe to be ideal in such situations. However, sometimes, we may have already started acting before we stop to think about the cause of our action(s). These are unconscious feelings and beliefs at work!

However, feelings and beliefs do not create themselves. They are formed from experiences at different stages of life. As we go through different experiences, we form different perspectives about life and the world, which get solidified in our minds as feelings and beliefs, which ultimately serve as the basis for responding to situations and circumstances. This connection between our experiences, our feelings and ultimately our behaviors reveals something crucial to influencing people.

To change people, provide a new experience that forms the kind of feelings you want them to have, in order to produce the behaviors that you want them to exhibit.

New experiences could either add to, take from, or modify our feelings and beliefs, and such changes determine the nature of the behaviors of that individual going forward. Therefore, to influence people, give them a new experience that is in alignment with the desired behaviors. For instance, a smart phone dealer will typically not bother you with excessive details about the features and potential of the phone. All they need you to do is to have a feel of the phone by yourself. By giving you the device, you're having a new experience, which creates a feeling, and this eventually determines the course of the behavior you exhibit.

So, the more you think in terms of the feelings and belief systems of other people, the more you are able to influence them.

A combination of thoughts, feelings, emotions, beliefs and behaviors is referred to as an 'attitude'. We can say that a person either has a good or bad attitude, but the truth of the matter is that what they are exhibiting is a simple combination of the five elements mentioned above. Understanding attitude is key to influencing other people.

CHAPTER - 17

CASE STUDIES OF

DARK PSYCHOLOGY

Joseph Stalin

Stalin was perhaps one of the most brutal and deadliest leaders of all time. Although he was renowned for harsh and terror-filled leadership, his tactics were not without some form of persuasion. Unlike other leaders who employed brute force from the inception of their rule like Idi Amin of Uganda, Stalin first reached out to the people with twisted half-truths to convince a certain portion of the masses to believe in his agenda.

Joseph Stalin's reign of terror left the people of the Soviet Union in debilitating fear. His form of mind control was almost unparalleled by any other leader. His foot soldiers carried out his orders without question and were even at liberty to kill, maim and punish anyone at will irrespective of whether they were guilty of any crime.

The citizens never knew when they would become guilty under any law because there was no law. Anyone could be sentenced to the GULAG (forced labor camps) for any reason. Getting out of GULAG alive held a slim chance. Even those who didn't suffer the ill-luck of being sentenced indefinitely to the GULAG didn't find living in society safe either. The masses were dying in droves due to starvation, murder or ill-treatment from Stalin's men.

How did the Soviet Union descend to this level of existence? What were the tactics used? Rhetoric! The Soviet Union yearned for a change in leadership. The people wanted leadership better than that under Vladimir Lenin, Soviet Union's head of government between the years 1917 to 1922. Stalin saw the gap and used the dark side of emotional intelligence to gain prominence in the heart of the people.

The people fell for his appealing talks, particularly the working-class citizens. They saw a future full of bright hopes and possibilities. However, what came after was far from the desires of the people. Stalin manipulated the people easily because he knew how to take glaring issues that would draw support from the people and combine it with well-timed emotionally-laden words that would trigger the right type of emotional responses.

Stalin was masterful in his use of emotional control even though he abandoned it for a more direct tyrannical method.

Adolf Hitler

German political leader, Adolf Hitler, was a type of speaker who spoke from the heart. He knew that to use reason would limit him to only a small part of the population. He poured his heart out in his speeches and that caused the people to become awestruck. Hitler mastered the art of persuasion and used it to negatively influence an entire nation into suspending their ability to think. They simply changed their perspective and acted without questioning Hitler's motives.

Hitler spent several years studying the power of human emotions and how body language can be used to effect intended emotional response. He would practice and analyze several hand gestures, facial expressions and other body movements. He used the power of body language to bypass the reasoning of the human mind and convey his messages directly to the hearts of the people. He worked very hard on developing and perfecting this ability. There is no doubting the fact that he mastered it.

When he finally began to deploy his skills, he would speak with so much passion that his voice seemed to rise from the depths of his body and penetrate the soul of his audience. His words fired up even the lazy and indolent. He could turn cowards and doubters into full believers in his ideas and philosophies.

Hitler was not born into an influential family. His rise to power was through sheer willpower and focused determination driven by his detest for Jewish people and the pain of his country's recent defeat.

Fueled by a feeling of depression at the state of affairs in his country, Hitler decided that the best course of action was to raise an army of people through mind-control tactics to wipe out his perceived enemies and put his country back on its feet again.

Using his masterful art of persuasion, Hitler didn't find it difficult making his followers kill other people for the simple "crime" of being from another race and religion. But if that wasn't bad enough, the people executing his dark agenda never felt they were doing anything wrong. That was the power of influence Hitler wielded over his followers—he made his followers believe in the rightness of their actions.

The result of all his indoctrination and propaganda through Nazi schools was mindless war. The Holocaust and World War II claimed the lives of over 40 million human beings.

CHAPTER - 18

UNDERSTANDING

DECEPTION

Deception is going to become dark any time when it is carried out with an indifferent or negative intention towards the victim. Dark deception is an understanding that the truth is not going to serve the deceptive aims of the deceiver. The deceiver is going to take the truth and either ignore, hide, or change it in favor of a version of events that suits their purpose a little bit better. Those who employ dark deception mean to do it as a way to harm, rather than to help. They want to help out their own interests, but they don't care who gets hurt in the process.

The Deception Spectrum

Deception can happen either on a small or large scale. Many people assume that deception has to occur on a large scale in order to be important. But dark deception is present in all parts of the spectrum, and it is important to be on the lookout at all times to ensure that you are safe.

Dark deceivers will often use the smaller deceptions to help them out as well. They may start out with some of these small deceptions in order to test out the victim and to condition that victim to believe the larger lies the deceiver uses later on.

Smaller deceptions can also be carried out with the goal of undermining the trust the victim has in their own powers of reason and logic. If the manipulator is able to deceive the victim over a smaller issue, and the victim starts to question what is happening, the victim may conclude that their suspicion is irrational, and they are not able to trust their own judgment. Most people will start to conclude that it is their own judgment that is at fault here, rather than entertaining the idea that someone else is deceiving them over some issue that seems so small. Of course, the dark deceiver is aware of this trust that people generally have and they will try to exploit it.

A dark deceiver can also work with a large-scale deception as well. One of the largest deceptions that they can use is to convince someone that you are someone else. Not in terms of just a personality trait or some other small detail. A true deceiver can even hide their entire identity. They will hide their date of birth, their name, and everything else. This is done in order to help push forward the goals or the agenda of the manipulator.

Deceptive Topics

Everyone has heard the saying "Money is the root of all evil." This may seem like an exaggeration, but money can often be the root of a variety of deceptions. Deception and money more often than not cross paths. Some people are going to deceive in the hopes of attaining money; others will do it to hide their money, and so much more. Because money shows up as a topic so often when it comes to deception, we are going to take a look at it now.

Take a look at a professional beggar. These individuals are going to try to get money from the public, even though they have plenty of their own. These beggars are going to use a few different dark psychological principles in order to get the money they want from their innocent victims. Such beggars are even willing to put some injuries on their bodies in order to look more desperate.

Personal marital status is another area where people are going to deceive. Sometimes, a person may try to hide their married background in the hopes of seducing a new victim. This could be for sexual or financial reasons. There are even other people who have multiple wives that are spread out across the world, wives who have no idea about each other. This deception type has become even harder with the beginning of the Internet and the ability to check in on people through social media. These deceivers can manage more than one wife from each other through many different means.

There are some people who may appear to be falsely married when they are not. A married couple is one that is often seen as more trustworthy compared to one that is not married. The dark manipulator is aware of this idea and may choose to use it for their own end goals. Some people may try to have a pretend marriage to help with taxes and insurance. One of the most common deception types with this is when the deceiver creates a fictional dead wife or husband in order to gain the sympathy of those around them and often their money.

A deceiver may also try to hide their own criminal background. This is because it is hard to be trusted, either personally or professionally, if you have committed certain crimes. Many manipulators feel like they can use deception in order to hide any socially unacceptable or abnormal feelings that they have. This can stop the victim from being alerted to the person they are dealing with until it is way too late.

For example, a dark manipulator may decide that they only want to use their victim for sex. But they know that if they focus on this topic, it is going to be a red flag and hard for them to get what they want. They then decide to deceive the victim. They may overtly lie and then imply that their true intention here is commitment and love. The victim is going to fall for this deception, the exploitation from that manipulator is done, and then the victim is the one harmed by the deception.

In a romantic relationship, the manipulator is often going to hide their true intentions. Deceptive actions and words are going to leave the victim feeling that the other person is exactly what they were looking for at that moment in time. The reason that this happens is that the manipulator is able to identify someone who is vulnerable and then probe into their needs and weak points. The manipulator is then able to use this information and then cloak themselves so they appear to be something they aren't. This is a common beginning with the manipulator that can turn into more long-term manipulations that the victim isn't aware of.

Deceptive Tactics

There are many different deceptive tactics that the manipulator is able to use at their disposal. Remember that this deception is the process of hiding information from the victim in order to reach their overall goals. There are four categories of tactics that fall into deception, and any given deception is likely to involve a blend of each of them, which can make it even harder for the victim to know what is going on.

The first deceptive tactic that can be used is lying. This is the first technique that the manipulator is going to choose as soon as they know that the victim is susceptible to lies and has trouble figuring out the truth. This is often because the victim is someone who trusts others. Or the manipulator may have worked on this victim for some time so that they lower their guard. The manipulator is also able to find ways to hide up the lies and then explain the discrepancies if the victim starts to notice.

Any deception that occurs with lying is likely to occur in a way that is very subtle and is thought out ahead of time. A deceiver is going to embed their lie into some information that is truthful. For example, the manipulator would start out with a story that is about ninety percent true and ten percent false. Because it sounds legitimate and most of the story can be proven as true, the victim will think the whole story is true.

Implying is another form of deception. Implying is when the manipulator is going to suggest something false is true rather than boldly stating it. If the manipulator wants to deceive a victim about how much money they have, then they could either lie or imply about it. A lie would be something like "Oh I'm a successful guy. I've made a lot of money," even though the manipulator knows this information is not true. But when they imply, they are rich, they may say something like "it's so stressful trying to handle things with my accountant. Trying to get my tax bill down takes a lot of my time." The manipulator has acted and spoken in a way that makes the other person think they are wealthy, but they never state it.

Omission is another option for the deceiver. This is a failure to mention something, usually a fact that is pretty important, that is true. Omission doesn't use a falsehood in order to cover the truth like the other two options. Instead, this one is going to ignore the truth or just leave it out. Often this piece of information is important for the victim to know about in order to make an informed decision. The manipulator would leave this out to protect themselves and ensure that the victim didn't have all the information.

One way that the deceiver can use omission is to create their own emotional fence with that situation. This is a tactic where the manipulator implies that a particular period of their life, or some particular topic, is painful or uncomfortable for them to discuss. The victim, feeling bad and wanting to be considerate, will avoid bringing up this topic. This gives the manipulator a chance to avoid the truth while still making the victim feel guilty when they try to bring up that painful topic.

And the final form of deception is going to be the most elaborate, and often criminal, form. This is known as fraud. Instead of the deceiver simply lying about something from the past, this kind of deceit is going to have false stories, documents, and some other evidence in order to back up whatever their lie says. The deceiver is going to use these things in a subtle way. They would never say something like "I'm a doctor; take a look at my certificate!"

Instead, they will use some subtle displays to show off to the victim. They will try to steer away from being too pushy with their fraudulent claims because they know that doing this will make the victim feel that something is wrong with the situation.

Fraud is becoming more common than ever because of the Internet. Deceivers can often work with some professional software in order to make documents that look pretty realistic, no matter what type of document they need. This can make it really hard to tell whether you are working with someone who is telling you the truth or if they are deceiving you.

When this dark deception starts to enter the realm of fraudulence, it can be a bad sign. It shows that the deceiver is dangerous and they are committed to sticking with that dark psychology. They are risking serious criminal charges to do this kind of manipulation, and they are confident that they are able to do this without anyone really noticing it at all.

CHAPTER - 19

WAYS TO PROTECT YOURSELF AGAINST MANIPULATION

There are so many things that you can do to protect yourself from the manipulation that you feel from another person. First, you need to avoid blaming yourself for the situation. The manipulator is never going to be one who will admit that they did something wrong. It is their job to feel as good as possible, and they will go through and make sure that you feel inadequate. In order to help them get what they want out of life, the manipulator is going to work hard to make you feel guilty and bad about yourself and everything.

During this time, remember that you do deserve to be loved and have dreams and goals. Remember that the other person, the manipulator, is trying to deceive you and make you feel bad, and they are not providing you with the respect that you deserve. You need to be able to stand up for yourself and fight off against this to get the results that you want.

Manipulators are often going to twist and change the facts because this helps them to come out the winner and come out ahead of everyone else. When you are responding to this distortion of facts, it is vital to seek out some clarification. Explain to them, firmly but respectfully, that you don't remember the facts that way, and that you want to try and understand what is going on. Being able to ask some questions can make a lot of difference.

Learning how to listen to yourself is going to help as well. Think about the way you feel about the situation at hand. Do you feel like you are free and happy, or do you feel like you are pressured and obliged to do things for someone when they ask? Does it seem like the other person is impacting you all of the time, and it is all going to be a big inconvenience to do the action for them, even though you have never wanted to do it? The answers that you can give to this are going to serve as a guide to where this particular relationship is heading, and if it is a good one for you to still be in.

You can also work to curtail some of the guilt trips that the other person is sending your way. This one is hard to work with, but if you can approach this, and not let the other person determine the situation and make the interpretation, then you will find that it is so much easier. You have to be able to take the words that the manipulator has said to you, and let them know that they are unkind, unrealistic, inconsiderate, and disrespectful to you along the way. Some examples of doing this will be below:

Yes, I know that right now, you are having some troubles. But it is not my responsibility to deal with this. I am not available after a certain time, and it is important that you call someone else if you think you need help.

I know right now; you are going through quite a bit in your personal life. But this doesn't change the fact that I need to go to work, class, and other obligations. Maybe it is better you talk with another person on some occasions, or even consider some of the resources that I have sent you on mental health instead.

I do care a lot about the hard work you have put in, and how you have been able to help me. I've said as that many times in the past. The problem right now is that you are not showing enough appreciation for how much I do care about you.

You can also learn how to focus all of the attention back on the person who is trying to manipulate you. Instead of allowing that person to ask you questions and be the one in control with the demands, you can take control over the situation that is there, and then turn it back on them. Any time you feel that they are pressured to do something that seems unreasonable, or you are not comfortable with, then you can ask them some questions that will turn things back on them.

And always remember that when you are dealing with a manipulator, you should never jump right into a quick decision without having the time to think it through. The manipulator knows that when their victim has to make some swift decisions, then they are going to end up making decisions that are not always in their best interest. Instead of just giving in and agreeing to it, it is much better if you can first tell the other person that you will think about it.

Of course, this is probably going to make the manipulator a bit mad at you for what they are doing. They want you to make that decision quickly because they know that if you have the time to think it over, you are going to say no, and not help them out with it. This means that if you ever feel like there is a lot of pressure that comes here, it is going to be a sign that someone is trying to manipulate you a little bit.

You may find that this is the perfect time to find your support group. Sometimes, a manipulator is going to try and isolate you from other people. This is because they feel that if they can get you alone, they will be able to convince you to do more things that you normally would not. If you focus on some of the healthier relationships in your life, and even start to build up some new ones, you will feel more happiness and confidence in the process. You can look at new friends, old friends, mentors, family members, and more. These are great to have because they are the ones who will help you keep the balance and happiness that is needed. And when that starts to show up more in your life, the hold that the manipulator is going to have over you will be gone.

And finally, it is often a good idea to stay away from the manipulator. If you find that it is harmful or at least difficult to interact with a specific person, it is time to distance yourself a bit more. Remember that your happiness, as long as it is not harming anyone else, is what is important, and it is never your job to go in and change the other person. If you find that the manipulator is someone you have to be around regularly, like a coworker or someone in your family, try to see if there are ways that you can safely and effectively limit the interactions that you have with them. It is best to only engage with that person when it is necessary.

Now, when you do try to separate from the manipulator, remember that they are not going to like this, and they are likely going to try and use all of the tools and techniques that they have at their exposure to help try to get you to stay. This means that when you do this, be prepared for the victim card, the smear campaigns, the guilt trips, and more. This is done because the manipulator is starting to see that they are no longer holding that control over you, and they do not like it. If you can hold out for a bit, rather than running right back, then you will be the one who wins.

CHAPTER - 20

PREVENTING

VICTIMIZATION

When you are able to recognize manipulators around you, understanding their most frequent behaviors and traits, and recognize that you may have some of the traits that manipulators find attractive, you can prepare to arm yourself against the manipulation through several different tactics. Each of these can help you develop the ability to stand up for yourself, proving to manipulators everywhere that you are not willing to be victimized and not willing to put up with their nonsense. By embracing some of these traits and lifestyles, you will make yourself much less desirable and much less manipulatable, which is usually enough to keep the manipulators at bay. After all, a difficult target puts the manipulator at risk for having his cover blown, something that no manipulator actually wants to see come to fruition.

Understand Your Rights

Perhaps the number one way you can defend yourself from manipulators is to recognize and understand your own human rights. When you are able to recognize your rights and what they are, you are then able to understand when they are being violated. When you are able to recognize when someone else is violating your basic rights, you will be able to stand up for yourself. Just by standing up for yourself and refusing to allow the manipulator the ability to do whatever he or she wants, you are going to deter the manipulator. You make it clear that you are not an easy target simply because you understand what treatment you are entitled to, and you are strong enough to enforce it.

Some of the most basic rights you have as an individual include the following:

- Right to respect: Every person deserves to be treated with respect. The catch here is recognizing that there are two fundamentally different ways the word respect can be used—it can mean that you are treating someone with basic human decency, such as recognizing the rights and boundaries of those around you, or it can mean respecting authority, as in listening to what someone who holds authority says you must do. These two types of respect are fundamentally different. You have a right to respect in the sense of being treated with human decency. Remember that the manipulator does not have the right to respect in regards to some perceived authority—he may have the right to human decency, but you do not have to obey what the manipulator says in the name of respect.

- Right to express yourself: You are free to have any thoughts, feelings, opinions, and desires you want to have. Of course, you are not free to behave in any way if it violates social norms, laws, or harms another person, but you are more than welcome to decide how you want to feel about a topic without anyone else having room to criticize your decisions. Remember this—oftentimes, manipulators like to try to strip individuals of their ability to think for themselves.

- Right to autonomy: Especially once you have reached the age of majority, you are free to be your own person. You are welcome to choose what you decide to make a priority as well as what you are choosing to consider a waste of your time. No one can tell you how you should spend your time without your consent, and if you are willing to stand up for your freedom of having your own thoughts and autonomy, the manipulator is going to get bored very quickly. If you are not open to his tactics, he will not waste his time when there are other people who will fall for his tricks much more easily without risking exposing himself.

- Right to say no: By and large, there is very little that you are actually required to do by law. Beyond paying taxes and ensuring that you are not infringing on the rights of anyone else, you are mostly free to do or decline to do, what you want. You are more than welcome to tell the manipulator no, and you should be free to do this without feeling any guilt about doing so.

- Right to take care of yourself: You should never be made to feel bad for taking care of yourself—ultimately, the only person who is likely to take care of you the way you will need is yourself, and if you cannot count on yourself to do so, you are going to find yourself and your health, both physically and mentally, suffering. This also means that you are free to protect yourself from toxic individuals—even if the manipulator is your mother, your sibling, your spouse, or even your child, you are well within your rights to stand up for yourself, even if that ultimately means that you cut off the other person if they refuse to respect your boundaries.

- Right to happiness and a healthy life:

Remember, everyone deserves happiness, and everyone deserves to be able to live a physically and emotionally healthy life. You have the right to this, and to creating your own happiness through all of the above. Even if the manipulator attempts to convince you that you do not deserve happiness for any reason, remind yourself that you do and refuse to let the manipulator put that thought in your head.

While most people will respect these rights without too much fuss, giving you the freedom and respecting your boundaries accordingly, there are people out there who would love nothing more than to steamroll over every individual right, depriving you of all of them in order to control you. Even if the manipulator tries to take advantage of you, remember one key fact: There are only strings involved if you let them be involved. You have all the power here—your own autonomy is your greatest asset, and if you refuse to surrender it, you will be able to protect yourself.

Stay Away from Known Manipulators

Another easy way to protect yourself is through sheer distance. If you automatically take some distance from the other person because you have a feeling that what he is doing may or may not be manipulative, you will protect yourself.

Manipulators require proximity, both personally and physically, to really be able to work their magic, and if you decline to give them that power, they will not be able to take control over your life.

Distance will also allow you to identify whether someone is actually the manipulator you may suspect him or her to be—with distance, you will be far more likely to be able to see whether or not the other person actually is a manipulator. From a distance, you can study the other person's behaviors when interacting with other people. You may be able to see the mood swings, such as shifting from being aggressive with one person, but playing the victim with another, if you are on the sidelines, avoiding detection.

Avoid Taking Things Manipulators Say to Heart

Remember, the manipulator wants nothing more than to break you down and exploit any vulnerabilities or weakness he or she may see within you. When they are able to recognize a weakness, manipulators often attack it with as much power as they can muster in order to break you down. Despite how difficult you may think protecting yourself will be, you have one key skill that will protect you—refuse to personalize.

Personalization is the idea that you take the blame for everything that is happening around you. If the manipulator is in a bad mood, you may naturally assume it was something you did, especially if the manipulator has taught you to have such a reaction. However, when you stop taking things personally, you are able to begin distancing yourself from the emotional reactions that the manipulator wants you to feel. He ultimately wants you to feel like it is your fault because guilt is something that can be easily exploited, and when he is able to exploit you through your guilt, you are going to be more within his control.

Along those same lines, recognize that you are not at fault here. It is not your fault that the manipulator chose to target you or attempt to target you, and you should not allow yourself to feel guilty for the actions of the other party.

Shift the Pressure onto The Manipulator

Oftentimes, those who are manipulative are far more willing to put unreasonable or unfair pressure onto their victims. They will demand things of you that would make most people balk, but nevertheless, the manipulator continues with his demands. They oftentimes will repeat these demands, growing aggressive in order to intimidate you into obeying. Luckily, there is one simple way that can usually take the wind right out of the manipulator's sails: Shift the pressure back.

If the manipulator asserts that you must go and run to three different stores to get the food for dinner that night because he has to have the tomatoes from store A, the cheese they offer in the deli at store B, and the specific cut of meat at store C, for example, you could stop and point out the inequity. The easiest way to do this is to ask deflecting questions that shift the pressure back onto the manipulator. A few examples of these questions include:

- "Is that really reasonable to you?"

- "Would you go out of your way to do all of this without complaint?"

- "Is this a request or an order?"

- "How does this benefit me?"

- "What about my opinion?"

- "Does this sound fair?"

- "Are you seriously expecting me to do xyz thing?"

These questions put the manipulator in a tough place—he can either say that yes, he does think what he is asking is fair, in which case he opens himself up to you requesting that he goes to do it if it is fair and reasonable, or he has to admit that no, it is not fair or reasonable to demand you to go and do whatever he has decided he wants.

While this method will work with several different kinds of manipulators, it does not work for everyone. Certain types of manipulators, especially those with the traits of the dark triad, may decide to completely ignore your attempts to prove their actions unjust and unfair.

CONCLUSION

We have come to the end of this fascinating discussion into the world of dark psychology and the various components which comprise the vast array of facets involved in this study. As such, thank you for making it all the way through to this point. We certainly hope that you have found information that is not only useful but also interesting to read.

Put the techniques that you have learned into practice out in the real world. Find a target that you want to manipulate and try some of your favorite techniques out, whether that means trying to control the narrative, attempting to manage your target's expectations, or making an effort to manipulate your target's beliefs. Do not expect to get everything right the first time, and do not be afraid of failure; if something goes wrong, simply learn what you can from the experience and move on to the next target. Learning a new skill is always a process, and that includes learning how to manipulate people in the world around you. If you feel that you have to, take a break from manipulation and come back to it at a later time. Frustration is never good for the learning process, and will only serve to make you want to give up altogether. As long as you keep trying, you will get there eventually. I know that I have repeated myself over and over, but remember that practice makes perfect. Once you practice long enough, you will find that you have mastered the techniques of manipulation and influence, and you will have very little difficulty in making targets bend to your will.

The practice is a great thing, but only when you are not enforcing bad habits instead of developing good ones. The best way to tell good from bad is to go back and read about whatever concept you might be struggling with, instead of letting bad habits take hold for the foreseeable future. We explored the various motivations that manipulators have for engaging in the activities they do. Moreover, we explored the reasons why manipulators act out in the manner they do.

Thus, here are the main takeaways from this discussion.

1. Generally speaking, manipulators have nothing personal against you. This means that a manipulator, when looking to take advantage of you, or any other victim, don't do it because they hate you, or have something against you. They do it because they have an agenda and will essentially look for anyone, they can take advantage of. If that happens to be you, then you need to address that issue before serious damage comes to you.

2. Manipulators are usually scared and often insecure individuals who look to prey on someone who is weaker than they are. This is something that you need to keep in mind especially when dealing with toxic people. For instance, bullies tend to be individuals who feel inadequate and will do everything they can to make others feel worse than they do.

3. Most manipulators seek validation and affection. In the particular case of narcissists, what they really seek is to be loved. They seek the attention and validation of those around them. However, their toxic attitude alienates them from actually getting what they way. In the end, they end up destroying any semblance of a meaningful relationship which could lead them to get what they desire most.

4. Guarding against manipulators is a lot easier than you think. However, it requires you to keep your eyes and ears open regularly. Also, keep an eye out for the red flags that we have pointed out. In doing so, you will provide yourself with a fighting chance. In the end, you will be better off while making it know to manipulators that you are no easy prey.

If you find yourself exhibiting any of the behaviors, that are consistent with manipulators, then it would be a great idea to make an assessment of what's really driving you to act in this manner. Perhaps there is something out there that isn't quite making you feel entirely comfortable about yourself or your surroundings. If that we to be the case, then perhaps seeking professional help may allow you to dig deeper into the root causes fueling your attitude. In the end, you may have the chance to develop a much more balanced outlook on life.

 Please keep these takeaways close to heart. As you gain more experience and knowledge in the topic of dark psychology, you will be able to further expand on them thereby achieving a deeper knowledge and understanding of this fascinating topic.

If you have found it to be useful and informative, please tell your friends, family, and colleagues about it. They too will surely find it to be useful and informative as you have.

CPSIA information can be obtained
at www.ICGtesting.com
Printed in the USA
LVHW050445251120
672446LV00015B/304

9 781801 123921